"What begins as a love letter to Italy transforms ever so gently into a beautifully cali-brated story of change, a seemingly simple journey—the awakening of the body, the mind, and the human spirit. Woven into this tender tale is a love story of two people who are so different and yet are perfectly fit for one another, each striving to transform the ordinary into something that is deeply meaningful. In the wise, capable hands of Angela Correll, every page delivers another lesson through a slice of idyllic Tuscan life."

—**Linda Bruckheimer, novelist, philanthropist, and preservationist**

"This is a terrific book. Angela Correll has given us an insightful, funny, and meaning-ful look at what it *really* takes to rebuild an ancient abode in a hilltop town in Italy: a very big heart. Whether buying mattresses, navigating the 42 steps it takes to gain a building permit, or just leaning out a bathroom window to take in the very best view of the Tuscan valley below, her observations on place, people, faith, and family make this book a treasure."

—**Bret Lott,** *New York Times* **bestselling author**

"*Restored in Tuscany* is a delightful and meaningful read. As I was caught up in the story of the restoration of an ancient building, I was also challenged by the possibilities of restoration in my own heart. May those who read this book find the flourishing life God has designed for every one of us."

—**Todd Harper, cofounder of Generous Giving**

"Angela breathes life into the journey from a small town in rural Kentucky to an even smaller hilltop town in rural Italy. Her gentle reveal is that although the tastes, smells, architecture, and landscape may be different, people are people, nature is nature, God is God, and marriage is a blessed gift as we navigate life. Her invitation is to join her and then make an unexpected journey of your own, to restore your soul and, in doing so, be an unexpected blessing to others."

—**Mark Rodgers, principal of Clapham Group and founder of Wedgwood Institute**

"Upon purchasing their home in Tuscany, Angela and her husband, Jess, pray, 'May God be honored, may it be a blessing to others, may we steward it well.' This wisdom applies equally to renovating a centuries-old villa and to anyone contemplating a course correction in the second half of life. Angela Correll's *Restored in Tuscany* is a refreshingly honest companion for those approaching a significant birthday ending in zero—or dreaming of buying a home in a foreign country. Italy viewed through a born-and-bred Kentuckian's lens, this is Correll's best writing yet!"

—**Matthew Sleeth, MD, author of** *Reforesting Faith*

"After polishing off the epilogue, which tasted like a perfectly paired after-dinner drink and dessert, I flipped back through page after page, longing for more. Such is the appetizing experience of Angela's new book, *Restored in Tuscany*. I was inspired to look for beauty in all of life as Angela's words painted images I could taste, see, smell, and feel. Her life's ups and downs and her celebrations and sorrows became gifts of healing for my pain and gratitude for my peace. Her mom was my mom. Her fears my fears. Her joys my joys."

—**Boyd Bailey, author, founder of Wisdom Hunters**

"This book is an invitation to dream and hope amid adversity. Infused with truth, vulnerability, and wisdom, Angela's words invite readers to take courage for our lives as we look over her shoulder and through her heart. We all have longed to have an adventure that changes us forever. I'm so thankful Angela wrote this book to give me the courage to dream again! *Restored in Tuscany* has completely engulfed me. I left encouraged to relish the moments of now and to never quit on my dreams for the future."

—**Ashley Marsh, hospitality designer and cofounder of Marsh Collective**

"I've been privileged to know Angela Correll and her husband, Jess, for more than two decades. Authentic, relational, committed, intentional, talented, and accountable—these words all describe this amazing couple. In *Restored in Tuscany*, Angela skillfully invites you into her life as she navigates painful losses. It is captivating! I couldn't put it down."

—**Howard Dayton, author, founder of Compass**

"*Restored in Tuscany* invites us into one woman's personal journey of restoring an ancient Italian home—but more importantly, it invites us into God's restoration of our hearts when we let him into the process. L. Mies van der Rohe said, 'God is in the details,' and Correll beautifully draws upon God's details in her well-designed abundance juxtaposed against the inevitable loss we all experience outside of Eden. This renovation story will leave you yearning to remake your own home, no matter where you are."

—**Margaret Philbrick, author of** *A House of Honor*

Restored
IN
TUSCANY

ANGELA CORRELL

HARVEST HOUSE PUBLISHERS
EUGENE, OREGON

The quotes on page 222 and 231 are from Tim Keller, "The Longing for Home," sermon, September 28, 2003, https://gospelinlife.com/downloads/the-longing-for-home-5328/.

Author is represented by Jenni Burke of Illuminate Literary Agency: www.illuminateliterary.com

Cover design by Studio Gearbox; Front cover photo by 6PM STUDIO; back cover photo by MeDisProject Photography, www.medisproject.com; cover art © AcantStudio (acanthus) / Shutterstock; cover flowers © Janmarie37 and © Agnes Kantaruk / Shutterstock

Interior design by Nicole Dougherty; Illustration on page 8 and compass on pages 233 and 238 by Brett Wiseman. All other interior illustrations © AcantStudio (acanthus) / Shutterstock

Photographs on pages 32, 151, 212, 227, 240 by MeDisProject Photography, www.medisproject.com, photographs on pages 37, 78, 85, 97, 104, 137, 139 by Angela Correll, photographs on pages 59 (bottom photo) and 228 by Gabe Osborne/FSNB, photograph on page 73 by David Puckett, photographs on pages 59 (top two photos) and 158 by Jason Asa McKinley. All other photography by 6PM STUDIO, www.6pmstudio.com.

For bulk, special sales, or ministry purchases, please call 1-800-547-8979.
Email: Customerservice@hhpbooks.com

Restored in Tuscany

Text copyright © 2024 by Angela Correll
Published by Harvest House Publishers
Eugene, Oregon 97408
www.harvesthousepublishers.com

ISBN 978-0-7369-8842-1 (hardcover)
ISBN 978-0-7369-8843-8 (eBook)

Library of Congress Control Number: 2023936846

Printed in China

23 24 25 26 27 28 29 30 31 / RDS / 10 9 8 7 6 5 4 3 2 1

To the

Montanini

CONTENTS

CHAPTER
N<u>o</u> 1

I look around as if I am seeing the inside of an airplane for the first time. That I am even on this plane is almost a miracle. I blink away the sensation of tears and, after a few minutes, realize my hand is still clutching our passports and boarding passes. I slide the documents into a side pocket of my carry-on bag, next to the bundle of Jess's paintbrushes, grabbed at the last minute. He didn't want to bring them or the paints and boards I stuffed into my suitcase; there will be no excuses now.

Time to relax, I tell myself. Nothing else can be done on this eight-hour flight, but I doubt my body or my mind will completely let go. We've been on guard way too long.

This trip can't possibly solve years of ingrained habits, but it might be the antidote for the weight of the last year, even for the busy weeks leading up to this moment. Or at least I can hope.

I rest my head against the seat and close my eyes, but my mind is spinning with thoughts and memories. For some reason, I need to go back to the beginning of this journey, not when we left the house this morning but earlier this summer, when the seed of an idea sprouted and tender roots curled into dry soil and changed the course of my parched summer.

"Thank you, yes, I'll be there." I listen to the details on the phone and write them down.

My laptop is open on the kitchen island while I add yet another event to an already overloaded calendar. I should be making supper, but there is always something else that needs doing.

My husband, Jess, glances over the top of our local weekly newspaper. "Did you say Mayfield? Long drive."

"Only an hour and a half. I can do the book club in half a day."

He puts down the paper. "You're thinking of Maysville."

"Yes, Maysville. Wait, no, Mayfield. Where is Mayfield?"

"Western Kentucky, near Paducah." He folds up the paper. "Do you want me to make supper?"

"That's almost five hours one way!"

He pulls pasta from the cabinet and opens the freezer door to hunt for our homemade pesto. "Not quite that far, but pretty close. You can call them back and say no."

"I accepted weeks ago. I can't back out now."

"Take Kristen with you," he suggests. "You'll like having company on the long drive."

"You don't have to make dinner. I can do it in just a few more minutes."

"It's okay. You finish up and I'll boil the pasta."

As the book club event approaches, I am torn. On one hand, I could use some time alone in the car after the frenetic activity of my first book launch layered over a full schedule of growing a soapmaking business and retail shop, along with the restoration of multiple guesthouses in Stanford, our little hometown in central Kentucky. Quiet time to sort out my straying thoughts.

On the other hand, Kristen is my intern, and I have spent very little time with her. I had reservations about taking on the responsibility, but she pressed for the opportunity to help with our hospitality businesses and the revitalization of our Main Street. It was hard to say no to cheap labor when we are all stretched so thin. My schedule is too erratic and unstructured for the consistency and shepherding an intern needs, so I assigned her to the store manager for the day-to-day operations, with me checking in from time to time. She is nearing the end of her summer internship, and I feel guilty about how little time I have invested with her. I invite her to go with me.

The conversation does make the trip to Mayfield go quickly as we catch up on her work with the shop and guesthouses and her many suggestions for improvement. We finally arrive and unload books at the public library. I am pleased to watch as a few dozen ladies and two men wander in and seat themselves around a U-shaped table. Their faces are eager and expectant, and they seem ready with questions and comments about the book.

Book clubs are some of my greatest joys. Writing is a solitary life, and to interact with readers who both enjoy my book and ask meaningful questions must be akin to a musician playing to an intimate and responsive crowd. The discussion time flies, and then we wrap up and say our goodbyes. Kristen and I find a place to eat a late lunch, with a strong coffee to go for the sleepy afternoon drive home.

Maybe it's our blood sugar dropping as the miles slip by, or perhaps the four-hour drive that seems to elongate like a race with no finish line, but soon a more negative tone takes the place of previous chatty conversation.

"What would you change or do differently?"

"To be honest, I'm disappointed in the internship," she says. "I wanted to work directly with you, not your managers. That's what I thought I was signing up for—to work with you."

I feel myself lean toward the steering wheel as if I've been punched in the gut. Why didn't I explain to her in the beginning that my time would be limited? While I am deeply involved in the operations of two of the businesses, I am also doing promotional events for my first book and trying to write a sequel.

Now that I'm thinking about it, why didn't I listen to my gut and tell her the timing is not good because I'm knee-deep in a renovation project to create an eight-room hotel? That venture alone has demanded much of my time.

Why didn't I consider saying no because I'm still grieving after the sudden, shocking loss of our son-in-law last year? Or because I want to be available to give extra attention to my widowed daughter and two grandchildren? Or because I have an aging mother who is becoming needier by the day?

Why didn't I pause and think about my summer garden that needs to be harvested and preserved? About how frequently we host people in our home in the summer?

Why didn't I consider how little I have seen my friends recently, how much I would like to have a day to myself for wandering antique shops or even puttering around the house in my pajamas?

And finally, why didn't I think about how little downtime I spend with my husband when we're not talking about the businesses? He always gets home from work before me these days. Just one night, I would like to be home first, to have the lights on, something delicious sizzling on the stove, and a candle lit.

My goodness, I am disappointed with how little time *I* get to spend with *me*, now that I think about it. My skin crawls with frustration, but getting defensive with this young woman is not the answer. I created this world in which I live—and willingly brought her into it without attempting to understand her expectations. The fault is mine. The truth is that I did have reservations about saying yes, but I plowed ahead, figuring it could be done, as if I have something to prove to somebody.

She is disappointed in me. I am disappointed in me. Who else am I letting down that I haven't heard from yet? And what the heck *am* I trying to prove?

"Can I get you something to drink?" The flight attendant leans over Jess and lists the offerings, interrupting my reverie.

"Sparkling water or club soda, please?" My throat is tight, but I manage to mouth the words over the steady hum of the jet engines.

She nods, and Jess confirms he wants the same. In a few small but focused motions, she creates our drinks and hands them to us.

"Thank you." I take a sip and glance at Jess. He is wide awake, engrossed in a high-body-count movie, his hand gripping the tray table, the drink ignored for the moment.

I turn away from him and look out the window. We are flying headlong into the night, leaving the sunset behind us. As the light dims, I fade back into memory, needing to parse out the steps that brought me here, now that there is time to think.

I stare at my laptop and rub my temples. My agent wants a draft of this second book soon, but headaches latch on with more frequency these days and sometimes stay for three days, like a rude houseguest. It's hard to think with a throbbing headache inside your brain, much less to write.

Research is done, I have a basic idea of the character arc and plot, and I have a fun idea for the setting. What I need is the time and space to work on it: to clear away the cobwebs of emails, requests, meetings, and decisions; to immerse myself in the place where part of the story will be set; and to have time to process my grief without having to be somebody or something for someone else.

Jess and I were in Italy only the year before when tragic news came to us. We had just arrived in Rome when we heard our son-in-law, Drew, was in the ICU. A precaution, our daughter Adrienne was told by the doctors, due to the chronic leukemia that had lain dormant in his body. So we drove tentatively on to the Tuscan countryside with the two couples traveling with us. We were in a van and bumped off the main road onto a gravel lane that wound into the Tuscan hills near Chianti. It was early afternoon when we pulled into the pebble courtyard of a charming boutique hotel made of stone mixed with stucco. Flowering plants softened the rock and the gravel, creating a cinematic scene that I captured in my mind and hold still. We had stumbled into some kind of paradise.

After a lengthy flight and then a four-hour van ride, we were ready to breathe in fresh air and take long walks around the countryside outside this quaint hotel. Our luggage was barely unzipped when our son called.

"You need to come home."

We flew home as soon as flights allowed and drove straight to the hospital to be with our family. Praying, sitting, hoping, and waiting for days, and then our son-in-law died. I know I cannot change what happened in those surreal and shocking days, but maybe a return trip to Tuscany can have a different ending this time.

A thought slowly blossoms in my mind like a frail and delicate flower, petals tender and craving the sun. I push back my laptop and tap my fingers over my lips.

That's the answer. I need a small Tuscan village where time stands still, where creativity can unfurl and my own soul can breathe. It will be good for us, and I can have space to write. A place where my character will live as part of a community.

Not the place where we heard about Drew's grave illness. No, this needs to be a new place, one not marred by death and bad news. The idea of a trip to Italy grows like a climbing vine, twining around my thoughts and unleashing a desire, maybe even a hunger, for time in a Tuscan village. Yes, I am convinced this is the answer, not only for progress on the book but for my own deep-seated need for rest. But there is another who must also be persuaded.

My husband is an entrepreneur gifted with a bright mind, artistic sensibilities, and a love for people. He has the ability to put together complicated deals like the puzzles he works in the wintertime. Along with these gifts is a natural curiosity to see what is around the next corner, especially when we travel, curiosity that can turn to restlessness when forced to stay in one place.

We have taken several trips to Italy over the years, but always as eager travelers, pedal to the metal from one end of the country to the other. Jess might be persuaded to stay in one spot for a week . . . but two? That sounds extravagantly slow. Yet two weeks in one place might be the antidote to the frequent tightness I feel in my chest, among a host of other symptoms.

I pick up my phone and google "heart attack symptoms."

Jess pushes open the screen door with his foot, balancing a tray with two glasses of wine and a plate of cheese. I drop the phone and look up.

"What is it?"

"Nothing." My left hand is still on my chest.

"Are you having another heart attack?"

"No!" I drop my hand and manage to sound offended. "That one wasn't a heart attack. It was a pulmonary embolism."

"It was pizza."

"Same symptoms." I reach for the tray and place it on the mosaic coffee table between us. Maybe it's time to test the waters. "I've been thinking about the next book."

"That's good."

"Yeah. It's been too hard for me to make space to focus on it here with all we've got going on. What about going to Tuscany this summer?"

"This summer?" The wheels are turning in his mind; he's thinking of the expense, of the two weeks away from business, time away from the farm.

"I need to finish the first draft by fall."

"Huh." He takes a sip of wine.

"I'd like to stay in a small village. A place where we can walk to the market

17

and to restaurants, so I can get a feeling for life there. I think two weeks would be enough time."

"You don't want to travel around?" He picks up a square of cheese and turns it over and over.

"I can't do that and write. I need to wake up in the same place every morning."

"How far along in your book does the trip to Italy happen?"

"About halfway through."

"Are you there yet?"

"You know I've only started." I try not to sound defensive.

"If you can write up to the point where you need the village, then we'll go." He pops the cheese into his mouth.

"We should go ahead and book the trip. Otherwise nothing will be available."

"We'll find something," says the non-planner in the family. "Do the work first, then we'll book two weeks."

I know he's trying to motivate me, but I already feel like the pressure cooker I use to can my green beans. A little pressure creates something good. Too much and the whole thing will blow.

Despite my misgivings, the next morning I'm pouring strong coffee at 5:06 a.m. I slide into my favorite club chair and prop my legs on an ottoman. I stare at the laptop for a few minutes, check the weather on my phone, then a news app to make sure no overnight disasters happened. Finally I open up the Word document and read again the notes I've written from my research.

By this time, my coffee mug is empty, so I get up and pour a refill. My little dog scratches at the mudroom door, wanting out. I let her outside, put food in her bowl, then let her back in. I hear Jess move around upstairs, so I scurry back to the chair so I can at least look like I'm writing when he comes downstairs.

"How's it going?" He looks at me with anticipation, as if I have morphed into Jan Karon overnight.

"It's hard."

"You're doing great," he says, and gives me an exaggerated toothy smile and a thumbs-up.

I'm not doing great, but I am in the chair with an open laptop. Like exercise, the first few days of a writing habit are painful until the muscle grows used to the work. I force myself to write one scene, then two, not having a clue if they're any good. The next morning, I only check the weather. This time I write a few more scenes. The following day, I write a chapter. After a week, I now look forward to putting myself in the chair and seeing what the characters will do. A migraine interrupts the start of week two, but I am back at it the next day, willing my fingers to type, even if I feel a bit wobbly. By week three, to my own amazement, the story is flowing.

The emails and to-do lists pile up, yet I am up early every day, writing furiously, putting everything else on hold until later in the morning. In the afternoons, I harvest the summer garden, and as soon as the supper dishes are whisked away from our farmhouse table, I can tomatoes and green beans in glass jars for the winter with Jess's help.

There are meetings that must be done for the shop and guesthouses in the midst of this, shadowed by the gnawing guilt over not spending enough time with my elderly mother. One morning when I finish my daily writing quotient early, I invite her to help me with the mass of vegetables on my kitchen counter. She readily agrees, to my great relief.

My little dog is happy to see my mother and welcomes her with high-spirited barks, despite being wary of her colorful painted Mexican cane. My mother's grand entrance is made with a red blouse, black leather pants, a cheetah print vest, and a hat that has more bling than a Vegas sign. All this for breaking beans.

I give her a hug and get her settled at the kitchen table. "Give me a pillow for the chair," she says. "I don't have any padding anymore." She eyes my backside as she says this, but before she can comment on my padding, I interrupt.

"Can I fix you a cup of coffee?"

"Black, two spoons of sugar." She says this every time, as if I don't know how she takes her coffee after approaching a half century of being her daughter. My mother introduced me to coffee as a child, mixed with a heavy dose of cream and sugar, and somehow it feels like our shared beverage.

Not only did Mom introduce me to caffeine at an early age, she also did not breastfeed, and she smoked during her entire pregnancy with me. It was a different time, but she was also a different kind of mom.

I stir the steaming coffee and get her settled at the kitchen table with a pillow for her chair. I spread newspaper and dump two bushels of Roma green beans onto the table. The pile is a foot high in the center, but my mother is a farm girl from way back, and she is not put off.

I dip bands and lids into boiling water to sterilize them while she snaps away at the beans and we talk.

"Nobody tells me anything anymore," she complains. "I have to check the Facebook if I want to know what my own family is doing."

"It's what people do now."

"Sarah's pregnant, did you see that? She better watch herself. Some girls take pregnancy as a green light to stuff their face. It's easy coming on, but it's hard to get off."

I know the pregnancy comment is not directed at me. I've never been pregnant; my three children were all teenagers when they came to me as gifts on the wedding altar. Still, this is dangerous territory. My mother has only come into her thinness in recent years as she has aged, yet she thinks she invented weight loss. Her diet plan involves coffee (two spoonsful of sugar) for breakfast, a decent-sized lunch of her choosing, cottage cheese for supper, and a bubbling finish with a Pepsi and two chocolate kisses for dessert.

I switch subjects and tell her about my writing progress, and that we are hoping to go to Italy for two weeks at the end of the summer.

"Humph." She grunts and then addresses my dog. "Maddie, Mama's gonna go off and leave you. What do you think about her?"

My desire to travel has caused tension with my mother since elementary school. I asked to go to Africa in third grade, to Copenhagen in fifth grade, and to Europe on a student trip in high school. The answer was always no.

Money was the main problem, but there was also the strangeness of it. If there was a little extra cash and a little extra time, we drove south to the Smoky Mountains in Tennessee or the beaches in South Carolina. We didn't go north or west. We especially didn't get on airplanes, and we most certainly never hurtled over the ocean in a metal tube.

⌘

"Chicken or beef?" The flight attendant is back, ready to hand me a culinary delight, freshly reheated in the galley.

"Beef, please." I scramble to unfold the tray table before she lands the cow.

I peel back the foil covering, and steam rises from the concoction underneath. As hard as it was to get everything caught up so we could go, and despite my mother's reservations, we are once again hurtling over the Atlantic Ocean toward a boot-shaped peninsula chock-full of history and art, with a cultural lifestyle I can only envy.

I take a bite of the beef and think back on how Jess was right after all. We did find a place to stay when I finally got half the book written.

"Are you sure?" the rental agent asked only a few weeks before. "It's a very sleepy village, only four hundred people, off the tourist trail."

I swirl mashed potatoes between the fork tines and add another bit of beef. *Are we sure?* At this point, it doesn't matter. We are on our way to an apartment we have never seen, in a village whose name we can't pronounce, in an area we don't know, for two weeks. There's not a thing to do now but give myself over to it and try to enjoy every minute.

CHAPTER

№2

We need coffee. Thirty minutes outside of Rome on our way to Tuscany, Jess steers the rental car into the parking lot of a roadside Autogrill. Inside the door, richly brewed coffee hangs heavy in the air. This is not American gas station cappuccino, with gushing powdered milk and weak coffee. The machines behind the counter could power a Lamborghini.

"Due cappuccini, per favore." Two cappuccinos, please. The cashier nods and hands me a receipt in exchange for euros. I lay it on the coffee bar and wait to be noticed. A barista takes my paper, reads it, and weaves between the other baristas in a choreographed dance to and from the gleaming machines. The air is filled with sounds of whirring, grinding, thumping, hissing, and the clatter of spoons on ceramic. It is the sound of hope, of new mornings and second chances. The cappuccinos slide in front of us, warm and foamy milk swirled on top and masking a stiff shot of espresso below. We stand at the counter and sip the hot liquid.

The coffee braces Jess for the drive and me for the ride. He grips the steering wheel like a professional Italian race car driver, but our Ford Focus is no match for the flying Mercedes,

Maseratis, and Lancias that whiz in and out of the narrow lanes. I release my white-knuckled grip on the armrest when we finally exit the autostrada, and Jess slows down to navigate curvy back roads. The landscape morphs from a green and blue blur into vineyards and olive groves.

A glimpse of stone and terra-cotta rooftops on a hilltop appears—and then, like a tempting mirage, it's gone. We meander another few kilometers, around more curves, and up the side of a small mountain. A tiny brown directional sign points the way to Montefollonico, and I feel a tingling of nerves race through my body. I've committed to staying in an unknown place to accomplish a lofty writing goal of half a book draft in two weeks. I hope this place is a fraction of how nice the photos online made it look, because there is no backup plan.

As we drive up a hillside, we pass a smattering of newer houses, a small school, and then the road seems to dead-end at an imposing stone entrance gate. Jess maneuvers the car next to a stone wall that borders a small park, while I crane my neck to take in all the surroundings. The shady park has slides and swings, meandering paths, a war memorial, and a bocce court.

Next to the city gate, old men sit like crows on a stone bench and stare at us with open mouths. Jess nods a greeting to them, and one gives an amused smile back, as if we are somehow on stage and he is surprised that we can see our audience.

Across from the city gate, *Bar Sport* is written in blue letters on a white plastic sign over the entrance to a coffee bar. Patrons gather in the garden outside for cards and coffee.

Just before the imposing arched stone entrance, but inside the great medieval wall that seems to circle the entire village, we glimpse an iron fence and a formal garden beyond. The overgrown garden has the look of a once-beautiful woman, now aging and dressed in faded clothes, but there is a story here, and I can't wait to discover it.

The entrance to the village is marked with a high stone and red brick gate, a section beyond where guards once stood watch, and connected to another

arched gate made with only stone. This double fortification now holds planters of peaceful geraniums, instead of soldiers with weapons. Tufts of green plants growing out of the wall in random places remind me of a man who rushed his morning shave.

Inside the village, the homes all have brown shutters—some open, some closed—and the houses are all connected to each other, roof to roof. Pots of all shapes and sizes, overflowing with brightly colored flowers, sit around the steps to front doors, and iron lamps hang from the sides of buildings.

There is a restaurant in the tiny piazza, tables and chairs under massive umbrellas, but it is quiet now, since we have arrived during the post-lunch afternoon rest. A small branch of the Monte dei Paschi bank, founded in 1472 in Siena and the oldest bank in the world, sits stately in the center, also closed. We stop for a moment and look at the documents the rental agency provided. While Jess studies the papers, I hear the clinking of dishes being cleared from a table. A gray tabby cat jumps off a windowsill to greet us. I have a sense we are being watched behind some of the closed shutters.

"This way." Jess charges toward a narrow side street. We pass another restaurant on the left with a quick glimpse of a jaw-dropping view off the back side of the mountain. On the right side, there is an art studio in an old chapel, the wooden doors latched shut. The street slopes down the hill and ends at another city gate, smaller and no longer used, with an iron pylon in the center to keep cars out. The gate serves as a frame for a stunning view of a hilltop village off in the distance, much bigger than Montefollonico. A small parking lot offers grace for those who mistakenly think this street will lead out of the village. Right before the parking lot, we find the address we are looking for. Climbing vines rise up from terra-cotta pots to wind around a string, placed just so, creating a glorious arch of greenery over the entrance, as if offering a glimpse of the care taken on the inside of the apartment as well.

We knock on the door and then ring the doorbell, but no one answers.

"Did she leave a number?" Jess turns to me, impatient. We have not slept in a bed nor had a shower for twenty-eight hours.

I dig in the papers the rental agency sent, worried that maybe I got the time wrong or, much worse, booked the wrong weeks. Still flipping through papers, we hear a door click from the neighboring house. A woman appears and looks toward us with a smile. No words pass in that instant, but I know she is coming for us and let out a breath of relief.

Wispy strands of dark hair have escaped to dance around her head, even though most of her hair is pulled back into a loose bun. Her pale blue skirt flows with the breeze as she walks, and her white cotton top flounces with movement as well. She appears to be in her forties, with soft folds of middle-age curves.

"I am Francesca." We introduce ourselves and shake hands. "How was the trip? Did you arrive in Italy today?"

We tell her about our travels and follow her inside and up the smooth terra-cotta tile stairs, worn from centuries of footfalls. At the top, another door opens into the apartment, where the tile floors continue. The ceiling, also terra-cotta, is held up by ancient wood beams. Papers are laid out on the dining room table, and I know we must conduct some business, but I can hardly keep my eyes from wandering around the room.

The dining room is dwarfed by a great fireplace large enough to sit inside—there are actually built-in seats with cushions to encourage it. As a teenager, I used to avoid my bone-chilling bedroom by taking Sunday afternoon naps stretched out in front of the fireplace. Even now in our drafty farmhouse, I often sit on a stool right next to the fire on cold winter nights. But *inside* the fireplace?

Francesca needs to show me *alcune cose*, or "a few things" about the apartment, so I focus on her as she demonstrates how to run the washing machine, the bedroom air-conditioning unit, and the dishwasher. Jess leaves us with the domestic details and fetches the luggage from the car.

When we are finished with the apartment tour, she turns to me and says, "If you need anything, I will be in my studio, next door."

Jess arrives and heaves our bags onto the top steps as Francesca bids us *arrivederci*. The door clicks shut and we are jolted with excitement.

There are three bedrooms, and we pick the one with the largest wardrobe I have ever seen, one that might lead to Narnia. I open it just in case it does, but I am already in some type of wonderland and there is no need to step through.

The apartment features an inviting living area with bookshelves and lamps and a small kitchen equipped with a gas stove, oven, sink, dishwasher, and a refrigerator shorter than me. Hand-painted tiles cover the counter and the stove vent, adding charming detail. From the kitchen window, a mountain is framed on the horizon, looking as if it might have been an active volcano at some point in history.

Jess pushes open French doors, and we step onto a covered patio with a bistro table, chairs, and a small settee. Beyond is another terrace with a larger table and chairs, and beyond that, a grassy garden with bushes, lemon trees in large pots, red geraniums, and a majestic palm tree.

For the moment, I am eager to empty our suitcases and hide them away for two weeks. Usually when we travel, our suitcases lie open with clothes stuffed and rumpled while we stumble over furniture in the night, hunting for the bathroom, which keeps moving on us. A tranquility floods me with the thought of staying in one place for two weeks. No hotels to book, no routes to plan, no packing and unpacking.

I lay the painting boards, brushes, and paints out on the dining room table. "Look what jumped into my suitcase!" I say, with a great show of surprise.

"No excuses, now," he replies, laughing.

∞

After unpacking, we visit the local market and fill our tiny kitchen with cheeses, salamis, fruit, tomatoes, garlic, onions, and bread. The delicate musky scent of peach is too much. I cut one and share half with Jess. Ripe peaches will forever remind me of our honeymoon, when we drove up and down Italy in a mad dash to see all the sites, gathering fresh peaches, cheese, and bread for our roadside picnics on the way from one city to another. I savor the sweet and tart flavor in my mouth and imagine it holds the promise of a second honeymoon.

I finish the peach, drunk on hope and anticipation, when a sobering thought crashes through my reverie. This may be paradise, but I am here to work. Half a book needs to be written in two weeks. I must prepare so nothing is left to chance. If my laptop isn't charged, I'll have to charge it in the morning. While I'm waiting, I'll get hungry and eat breakfast, which will make me sluggish, so I'll need a walk. Which will make me sweaty, so I'll need a shower. Time for lunch, then a nap, and before I know it, the day will be gone, and I'll sink into a miry pit of guilt and self-doubt as I realize I have lost one of only fourteen days.

I set my alarm for an early hour, charge the laptop with an Italian adaptor, and prepare the moka pot. The moka pot is a brilliant Italian invention from the 1930s that makes espresso coffee on the stovetop, much like our old-fashioned percolators but smaller. Despite its petite size and cuteness, it bubbles an espresso-style coffee that packs a wallop. I don't tamp the coffee basket quite as dense as the Italians, which makes it a little less potent. That most important task done, I try out the terrace settee, add some cushions, position the ottoman, and bring a table around to the side for my coffee. I put my hands on my hips and study the space. It is good.

Jess is in the tiny shower upstairs, so I run water in the bathtub for myself in the other bathroom, flinging open the window to the street below as I wait for the tub to fill. The golden afternoon light floods the room, which features the bathtub as a centerpiece, and the open window affords a fine view outside. I ease into the hot water and feel the travel tension melt away as if the bath is a final welcome, a cocoon of anticipation.

While this washing is nothing to a sacred baptism, when I rise from the water, cleansed and renewed, my spirit senses something beyond the physical.

Writing may be the reason Jess agreed to this trip in general and to staying in one place for two weeks in particular, but if I am honest, I am here for a reason much deeper than writing. I can hardly identify this desire—or is it hunger?—for something I sense this place has for me. Is it simply two weeks of resting my body and mind among the ancient stones and the beauty of the landscape? Or is it a much deeper soul-filling restoration that I crave, the kind only God can provide?

My hands and heart are open.

CHAPTER

№3

Ernest Hemingway had the ideal writing schedule, and it's one I've tried to imitate—minus the whiskey-swilling late nights and marriage-busting affairs. He worked in the morning hours, leaving the rest of the day for pursuits and people, both of which informed his writing when he went back to the desk. After four hours of writing, stepping away usually helps me process what I have written and think about what is coming next.

While the idea of this schedule is my goal, in reality I have faced obstacle after obstacle to writing. In the ten years it took to write my first book, some time was spent simply taking classes in an effort to learn fiction writing, but there were also multiple laptop crashes and other technology challenges, family crises, long illnesses suffered by those I loved, deaths, house remodels, and countless overnight guests who needed conversation in the mornings along with coffee and breakfast.

I've fought doubts, rejection, and a strong desire to chuck my writing into the nearby lake. I've experienced a nearly magnetic pull toward other responsibilities, especially those that have an easy start and finish. After all, a book can drone on with no end in sight, but a dishwasher has start and end cycles.

Through it all, the decision that I cannot live without writing guides my perseverance and keeps me opening the laptop and opening my mind.

Despite my preparations the day before, I expect more difficulties when I ease into the settee on the porch that first dusky gray morning in Tuscany, but I dive in anyway. I reread all of what I have written so I can get myself into the minds of the characters. Then I begin with new writing, only a few sentences at first, but within a couple of hours I am back into the story and infused with the excitement of being in a new place. The story is flowing with no hitches.

In between bringing me cups of coffee and breakfast, Jess has been studying the guidebooks and has a plan for our afternoon outing.

"Where are we going?" I am happy not to make decisions after taxing my brain for hours.

"Let's drive toward Pienza and then the valley beyond, toward the

mountain. It's called Amiata, and you're right, it is a dormant volcano. There are hot springs all over this area." His voice is excited. I have kept him pent up long enough; he is ready to explore.

Pienza smells of the pecorino sheep's milk cheese it is famous for, a tradition brought over by Sardinian immigrants, but it's so much more. Pienza is an early Renaissance town and a UNESCO heritage site, known not only for its historical center but also for the sweeping views of the Val d'Orcia beyond the Cathedral of Santa Maria Assunta.

This valley has attracted painters and artists since the Renaissance who have often tried to capture the bucolic landscape featuring wheat fields, olive groves, vineyards, and *crete senesi*, or the "clays of Siena," which look like landslides of gray gravel from a distance. Vivid green cypress trees contrast with the flaxen fields and line white gravel roads that curve in and around hills from one village to the next. The peaceful scene before us is inspiring, and we stand for several minutes, simply taking in the creation as if it were a sacred piece of art.

When the spell is finally broken, we walk until we find a restaurant with outdoor seating and twining vines in terra-cotta planters to shield the diners from passersby. *Pici* is the local pasta, we are told, and are served a thick spaghetti, hand-rolled and delightfully rustic. Jess takes his with wild boar sauce called *cinghiale*, and I choose a flavorful tomato sauce.

After a bottle of sparkling water and an espresso to finish our meal, we leave Pienza to explore deeper into the Val d'Orcia by car, lured by the view. I roll down the window so the scenery is even more vivid as we drive slowly, turning our heads from left to right so nothing is missed. The dry heat feels healing compared to the life-draining humidity we have in the summers at home.

A pile of stones lies before us, tucked under a hill. Jess pulls over and I know we are about to traipse through weeds and brambles to see the remains of an old farmhouse. This has been part of our relationship from our second date, this curiosity about what once was and what could be, a shared wish to see what is ruined be redeemed. Signs warning people to keep out have never deterred Jess, and I have always followed along after him, albeit with a great deal more trepidation. Here, there are no signs discouraging visitors, so to us, it seems an open-door invitation. Despite being in sandals, I won't be left behind. I don't want to miss a single treasure on this trip.

We climb on the stones like goats, calling out discoveries to each other as we spot what might have been the entrance of a former garden area. We have tackled some big projects in our tiny historic town, but all our renovations had roofs and four walls and were no more than two hundred years old. This is far beyond our cache of experience.

"Can you imagine taking on this pile of rubble?" I stand on top of a stone, hands on hips.

"It will take a pile of money, I can tell you that."

"I hope someone does it someday." I feel a bit wistful for this heap of stones, knowing it can be so much more.

"I'm glad it won't be me."

I carry my notebook with me everywhere we go, especially in the village, so I can take notes about places my characters might go for scenes in the book, the food they eat, and the way light plays on the honey-colored stones of the buildings and walls during different times of day. My writing is flowing as I had hoped, and we are coming to know the rhythm of the village and our routine within that rhythm.

Most of the morning village activity we observe is from our bathroom window, the only window that faces the street. Between cups of coffee and short breaks, I stand at the window and take in the view of the distant hilltop village I now know is Montepulciano, veiled under a summer haze, but I also watch for the comings and goings on the street below.

The mornings are alive and fresh, and I feel compelled to linger a few minutes for this "research." The window faces the pedestrian-only gate down the hill that leads to hiking trails and a church we never see anyone enter. Dogs are walked, greetings are called, and laundry is hung. We regularly see an elegant woman, perhaps in her seventies, take her dog out for a short walk, but it seems she disappears into a large wooden door in the wall.

This window to the village is a novelty to me and so unlike my view on the farm. Houses and gardens are connected here, sometimes meandering in and out of each other, just as the lives are connected with each other. But even more than the window, I enjoy the walks in the village so I can press images into my mind for writing later. I scribble notes about the details I take in on these walks and also during lunches and dinners, cappuccinos at the bar, and by watching the Italians as they talk to each other on the street. I won't use every detail, but the more I can bring a reader into a scene, the more invested they will be in the story. And when I observe details for my readers, it brings me more into the present moment as I search for words to describe what I am feeling, thinking, and experiencing.

I have noticed how the old men walk up the street, leaning into the hill, with their hands gently grasped together behind their backs. I think about how one of my characters, a seventy-year-old resident of the village, will walk up a hill in just that way. I think about my own father, gone now for several years, and I can't imagine him ever slowing down enough to walk like that. He pumped his arms, rushing from place to place, and even when he tried to slow his pace, he still walked with purpose. I have taken after him and naturally have a fast pace. But this walk is meditative, reflective.

As Jess and I start up a hill one afternoon, I put my hands behind my back and practice walking like the older men. I am surprised by how the simple act balances me as I climb the hill. It forces me to take measured steps, but in a way that gives my body a sense of harmony. It is a discipline for me since I am much more comfortable with swinging arms.

We are close to our apartment at the end of our exercise when the elegant blond woman walks out on the street with her dog.

"I wonder what her story is."

"Let's introduce ourselves," Jess says, picking up his pace.

"She may not speak English."

"She does," he calls back over his shoulder. While he forges ahead, I turn the key in our apartment door lock but then make my way to the bathroom window so I can watch, unobserved. As I position myself for the best view, they both turn toward the apartment, and I am forced to wave back with no way to explain why I am hanging out the bathroom window.

They continue chatting for a few more minutes before parting. Seconds later, Jess bounds up the steps to the apartment.

"Her name is Benedetta and she has invited us for an *aperitivo* at five o'clock Saturday to see her garden."

"How did that happen in the five minutes you talked with her?"

He looks at me blankly and shrugs. It's a mystery to him as well, this gift he has with people.

After my writing session the next day, we set out for a lazy drive on the *strade bianche*, the many white gravel back roads that weave throughout Tuscany connecting village to village. The white roads are dusty with no recent rain and send up clouds behind our car and onto the grapes near the road; they will be washed clean during the next rain.

The road is often separated from the olive groves and vineyards by tall cypress trees, standing like guarding sentinels on both sides, trunks clad in chalky white from the road dust.

Jess slows the car and then stops. In front of us lies a landscape that looks like a three-dimensional painting from an old master. Yes, a very old master indeed.

Grassy green hills rising on both sides of the white road contrast with the dark green of the cypress and the white gravel. We stare silently for a few moments.

"Can you take a picture of that? I might try to paint it."

I look at him sideways with a grin, but he doesn't meet my eyes.

"I said *might*." But I see a twitch play at the corner of his mouth.

Outside the car, I take several angles so he can choose the best one, then show him what I've taken. He approves, and we continue our slow drive and approach a vineyard where full grape clusters are ripening on the vine, soaking in the last weeks of maturation before harvest.

"What happened here?" Jess slows the car again. At first, I don't understand, until he points. "Look on the ground."

Plump clusters of ripe grapes lay scattered on the ground below the expertly pruned and trained vines, all the way down the lengthy rows. He pulls over, and we get out of the car to take a closer look.

"Maybe they're coming through later to gather these."

I bend down and pick up a cluster to examine it more closely. The grapes are perfect, and there seems to be no reason for them to be cut from the vine.

Two men are working across the road, and between our broken Italian and their fragmented English, along with a good dose of sign language, they tell us that for every three clusters, a fourth is cut off, which results in the production of the best quality of wine.

Back in the car, my mind goes to the Scriptures where Jesus talked about pruning, but I never envisioned that meaning healthy and ripe fruit. My only pruning experience is with my blackberry bushes at home: I cut the deadwood

in February so the new growth has room to bloom. Besides the health of the plant, it helps the aesthetics as well, but I'd never considered cutting a branch with fruit. It seems like such a waste.

This idea is something to ponder. While the image of the good cluster of grapes lying on the ground is thought-provoking, I find it also slightly haunting. Are there good and flourishing things in my life that are keeping me from the best?

A significant birthday is around the corner. Maybe it's time to think about my life like this vineyard. I know I must first cut the dead branches that serve no purpose, like my blackberry bushes at home. Then I can envision cutting the green vines that trail off in directions that suck energy from the purpose of the plant. But the good fruit? That will take courage.

∽

Jess has squirreled away his painting supplies into the upstairs room with a small window that offers good light. He paints in the late afternoons, in the gloaming hours before we go to dinner, spending far more time there than I imagined when I brought the painting supplies.

On this evening as we prepare for a dinner out, I climb into a bubbling bath and let the warm water envelop me. The days seem to be taking wing, and I am surprised to realize we are nearly halfway through our trip.

After his painting session, Jess showered in the tiny upstairs bathroom and now stands naked in front of the sink in the main bathroom, studying his face in the mirror as he shaves.

The bathroom window is open, allowing fresh air to fill the room. A television blares from the house catty-corner to us, and I imagine that my sloshing around in the bathtub can also be heard from the street.

With the soft evening light from the window casting an ethereal glow around him, Jess now appears to me as the model for a marble statue, possibly carved by Michelangelo's own hand. He finishes shaving, unaware of my eyes on him or that I have just pictured him as a Renaissance inspiration. He leaves the room to dress for dinner.

I grab a towel and wrap myself up in it. I stand in the bath, fully visible from the street through the bathroom window should someone look up, but no one is there. For now, the street is empty, part of this village rhythm that has gone on long before we arrived, for hundreds of years, in a cadence and pattern of lives lived in the beauty of this place and upon this mountain. I am only a traveler, experiencing a taste of it for a short moment, but what a gift to be here, savoring this time.

The morning haze is gone now, and the evening light is washing Montepulciano in brilliant reds, golds, and pinks before the setting sun dips below the horizon, one final good-evening kiss. I can imagine the warmth emanating from the stones in the afternoon light, but it can't possibly be any warmer than I am feeling inside my heart at this moment.

Buonasera.

CHAPTER
N⍛ 4

Benedetta's garden can be entered through her apartment or through the curious wooden door that faces the street. Because it is our first visit, she takes us through her comfortable apartment. There is a picture of her as a young woman riding a horse, pictures of her with her husband and family members. Books are everywhere, and so are cozy nooks for reading. Her small dog greets us and sniffs until she decides we are no threat. The door to the garden is open, framing a world of beauty created with trees, plants, hedges, and architectural features.

There is a fountain with crumbling mosaics and, next to it, a grand cistern filled with water that must be thirty feet deep. Vines climb up the crumbling palazzo wall, as if placed with artistic precision.

We look over the railing of the upper level and see the rest of the garden that eludes us from the small view from our apartment yard. It is filled with weaving patterns of boxwood plantings, round fountains, lemon trees, palm trees, and a shady area at the end with benches and statuary.

Benedetta tells us about the history of the garden, how it was created in the 1800s by a landscape designer. Our landlord, Francesca, arrives and joins us as we go down the steps and into the garden. We walk the length of it, and Benedetta shows us the historic laundry area, now taken over by hundreds of sleeping bats. We visit the *limonaia*, the place where the lemon trees go in the winter for protection.

The garden deserves more than an hour tour—it needs slow and thorough appreciation, time to sit and reflect, time to watch the water gurgle from a fountain and to see the shadows lengthen and shift. Time for prayer and time for silence. The creator anticipated this kind of use, rather than quick tours, but I am happy for what I can take from it, even as it creates a longing for more.

We walk back up the stairs and seat ourselves around a garden table in the shadow of the stone palazzo. Benedetta resists our offers to help and disappears into the kitchen, reappearing minutes later with a tray of snacks and drinks.

I wasn't sure what to expect for an invitation to *aperitivo*. Before us is laid a selection of cheeses, potato chips, and olives, along with a bottle of prosecco, another white wine, and sparkling mineral water. This seems an ideal way to entertain; the stress of an entire meal is removed, and the focus settles on friends, conversation, and beautiful weather.

We are chatting and nibbling when a turtle appears from around a corner and heads with surprising speed toward my feet.

"Watch your toes," Benedetta warns. "Leonardo will bite the toes."

He is opening his mouth to latch on when I move my feet, not a moment too soon. Benedetta fusses at him in Italian, picks him up, and walks him around the side of the cistern. I am wary and keep one eye open for him. I am generally an animal lover, but a toe-biting reptile is another matter. When Benedetta returns, she tells us that she has had the turtle much longer than the dog—twenty years, to be exact.

We bid goodbye to our lovely and interesting hostess and extend a dinner invitation for later in the week to both Benedetta and Francesca. We have made friends.

∞

The next day, we notice an unusual hum of activity in town. A table is being set up that stretches from the piazza to the market, and the smell of sizzling garlic and roasting meat hangs in the air.

"What is going on?" we ask Francesca when we stop by her ceramic shop.

"*Ferragosto*." When our faces show a lack of understanding, she tells us August 15 is an Italian holiday celebrating a day of rest after weeks of hard work, similar to our Labor Day. It is also a celebration of the Assumption of Mary, and services are held in local churches to mark the occasion.

Since we have not been invited to participate in the festivities, we make our own dinner plans. I propose the less-than-promising restaurant up the street, the one with pictures of the food on the board outside and the wrinkled AstroTurf viewing platform to the side.

"The view is worth a bad meal."

"I don't know." Jess eyes the refrigerator, which still holds a plate of cured meats from the market, or what the locals call the *alimentari*.

"How bad can a meal be in Italy?"

"Whatever you want to do." It is faint agreement, but I take it.

We are the only patrons, so we have our choice of seats. I pick the terrace, and we are seated and brought water. We both select simple pasta dishes. This is not the time to be adventurous.

Orders placed, we walk to the edge of the wall where the flat Val di Chiana stretches out before us forty miles or more, so unlike the rolling hills of the Val d'Orcia on the opposite side of Montefollonico. Cortona is across from us, a Christmas tree shape on the side of a mountain on the other side of the valley. Lake Trasimeno, in the neighboring region of Umbria, is off to the right, where Hannibal's army ambushed the Romans in 217 BC. To the left are the majestic Apennine Mountains, far behind Arezzo. Cars zip back and forth on the A1 autostrada, while a train follows a similar trail, both splitting the valley into two parts. The view is filled with so much history yet teems with modern life. We watch as shadows shift and daylight edges into dusk.

I could stand here at the terrace rail and take in the scene all night. The food is fine after all, but it was simply an admission fee to the real show. Glimmers of lumination grow brighter as night slips over the valley like lights dimming in a theater. Cortona sparkles in the distance like a diamond-studded brooch pinned to the side of the mountain. Before leaving, we take one last lingering look from the wall now that darkness has claimed the day.

Jess and I lean into each other on our walk back to the apartment, quiet in our thoughts and contented reflections. A din of conversation emanates from the piazza, and we are drawn by the boisterous chatter.

We pause, hand in hand, watching the villagers laugh and talk with neighbors and friends as they break bread together seated one next to the other on benches at communal tables. I feel a surprising desire for a seat at one of those tables.

∽

There are only a couple of days left before we must leave for home. Two weeks seemed like a glorious luxury of time, and yet it is nearly gone. Despite this, I feel a deep satisfaction with the progress of the book. It is nearly done.

Tonight, we are taking our new friends Benedetta and Francesca to dinner at Il Mulino, a restaurant outside the village wall and down the hill. Francesca is dressed in layered cotton shirts and her signature long flowing skirt, looking every bit the free-spirited artist. Benedetta is wearing a white jacket over a blue top and white pants, all slender elegance.

Even though it is walking distance, it's straight down the hill, which means a hard climb after dinner in the dark, so we decide to drive and pick up both ladies at the palazzo. The restaurant is in an old olive oil mill with vines draping the stone building like a cozy blanket.

When we arrive, we are seated at an outside table under the horse chestnut trees, overlooking a view of Montepulciano that is slightly different from the one I see from our bathroom window. We came to this restaurant our first week here, when I furiously scribbled in my notebook, making this exact table a scene in the book.

Our waiter, Roberto, reminds me of a character actor in a Hollywood movie with his square jaw and thick head of hair. He tells us about the mushrooms, how difficult it is to get them—but behold, a miracle has been performed, and they are in the kitchen tonight and ready to be made for us.

Carlotta, the owner, appears to welcome us, clothed in black stiletto pumps and a sparkly black dress covered by a matching sparkly black apron. We quickly see she is good friends with both Benedetta and Francesca. They chatter away in Italian, throwing in a word or two in English as a courtesy to us.

I find out at dinner that Carlotta and her husband have been divorced for quite a long time now, yet they continue to operate the restaurant and hotel together. Even more surprising is the fact that Carlotta is the chef, and she will be cooking in those stilettos.

We must certainly have the mushrooms, along with Carlotta's pasta, followed by sliced beef we can share. Then our wine order is placed—after the food selection, of course, because Italians cannot fathom how one could possibly know what wine to order until the food is chosen.

I go inside for the restroom and find yellowed newspaper and magazine articles about Carlotta and her husband when they were married. They had a Michelin star in the past. Photographs hint of the glory that once was.

The meal is delicious, and the mushrooms truly are quite special. After dinner, Carlotta appears again. Her blond hair and red lipstick are still perfect. She receives our compliments for the dinner, chatters again with Benedetta and Francesca, and shimmers away into the night.

We drop Benedetta and Francesca off, park the car, and walk back to our home away from home. The glimmering stars above remind me of the sparkles on Carlotta's black dress.

"How do you work in a hot kitchen, dressed like that, looking like she does afterward?" I wonder aloud. I think about myself when I am in the midst of canning season: hair in a ponytail, no makeup, tennis shoes, and usually smudges of blackberry jam or tomato sauce on my shirt.

"She's Italian."

∽

The following morning, I rise early to write with a bittersweet feeling. It is the day before our last day in Montefollonico. I finish the last chapter of the first draft of my novel, *Guarded*, hit save, and close my laptop.

"It's finished," I say to myself, reflecting on the last two weeks and the miracle that I actually wrote half a book here. There will be many more revisions to come, but a first draft is something to celebrate.

"You're done?" Jess stands in the doorway, a plump peach in his hand. I reach for my phone and hit play, and Handel's "Hallelujah Chorus" erupts. We dance on the patio, taking bites of the peach and letting the juice run down our chins.

We have heard about a very good restaurant in Monticchiello and decide to go there for a celebratory dinner. We take the slow route on the gravel *strada bianca*, savoring our last drive through this countryside. We pass the vineyard where the grapes were cut and see them still lying on the ground, shriveled from the heat and sun. I think about the quality of wine that will be made from the remaining clusters and wonder how fine this wine must taste.

Beyond the vineyard, we crest a hill and are stopped by a caravan of bobbing white fluffs of sheep as they cross from their field to the safety of their barn for the night. A young woman and a young man herd them gently, mainly by simply being present, since the sheep seem to know this routine. But there's always a chance one could go its own way, despite the lure of safety and food over the next hill, so the shepherds are there with staffs to gently prod them toward home. Tinkling bells and bleats add music to the air as we turn off the engine and roll down the windows to take in the sights and sounds.

The farmer in Jess admires the animals, their health and conformation. I see the way the shepherds, present in body and voice, treat the sheep gently with the goal of protecting them. My mind drifts to the many parables Jesus told about shepherds and sheep, and vineyards and grapes. Although living on a farm gives me a certain understanding of the agricultural parables, the stories told by Christ seem even more real in Tuscany, here where vines and olive groves line the hillsides, fig trees are heavy with ripe fruit, and sheep are guided across dusty roads.

$$\sim\!\!\infty$$

The next morning after coffee, I pull out the suitcases, hidden in the dark of the armoire for two weeks, and begin to pack. We take a final walk around Montefollonico, bid our new friends goodbye, and for dinner cobble together a monkish meal from the scraps of leftovers in our fridge. We rise early on the morning of our departure, and Jess heaves the luggage, now filled with olive oil and wine in a desperate attempt to take Italy home, down the stairs.

With one foot in the car, I glance back at the bathroom window where we viewed our Italian world, and tears spring to my eyes. Montefollonico was everything I hoped it would be and even more than I dreamed.

Montefollonico is Francesca, Benedetta, and Carlotta. It is the changing sunlight, the foamy cappuccino, and the ripening grapes.

It is the place where love is rekindled and I am present in each moment, pressing details into my mind. Where new colors are vivid in the sun setting beyond the mountain and where fluffy white sheep bob over gravel roads. Where the soul is fed, where shepherds prod their sheep, and where vines are pruned.

It is where I see myself anew, what is most important, and the things that must be done so that my own vine can thrive. If I flourish, then I can offer my best to others.

Let me guide you through this pruning, I sense the Shepherd gently whisper.

CHAPTER
N<u>o</u> 5

As time goes by, lessons from those glorious two weeks in Italy fade while the vivid memories do not. It's hard to undo a lifetime of habits and an engine that is made to run in high gear. Thoughts of incorporating rest into my daily life are engulfed by daily needs of the book and the downtown shop and guesthouses. I experience a certain type of comfort when I'm fully engrossed in activity and work, and I cling to it because it is familiar. After all, I've been working since I was a child. It's a family tradition.

One of my father's older brothers, Addison, was a successful real estate broker and auctioneer; he owned a real estate company in a neighboring town. He mentored my father and encouraged him to get his broker's license. When my father passed the test and received his license, he hammered a sign into our small front yard and Crouch Real Estate, branch office number two, opened for business.

An ad ran in the local newspaper announcing this expansion and our service model: "Call us day or night. Serving you is our main concern. Make us prove it." Our home phone number was the business number, and now we all three had to answer, "Crouch Real Estate, how may I help you?" day or night.

I was seven years old and had my first job. This was my father's second job and my mother's third. My father's full-time work in the maintenance department of the state hospital for mental illness meant he showed houses in the evenings and on weekends. My mother worked two part-time jobs serving in the elementary school cafeteria and as a crossing guard. Now she became the secretary for the real estate office, and I was her backup.

We lived in a tiny four-room house in a former railroad community in what is known as West Danville because it is literally across the railroad tracks from Danville proper. This was the house my parents bought after moving out of a tenant house on my grandfather's farm. Though small, it had indoor plumbing and central heat, important upgrades from the tenant house. Both my parents had the loss of youthful marriages behind them and three adult daughters between them. Marrying each other and having a baby was a new beginning, but one that came with no financial padding except for what they built together, which was a motivation for hard work.

Since there were only four rooms and our living room was now a real estate office, Dad hung Western-style saloon doors between the living room and kitchen to keep our kitchen and bedrooms private, doors that snapped back with a whack if you weren't careful walking through them.

Between her three jobs, my mother studied hard for her real estate license and eventually joined Dad in our business, first as a salesperson and later as another broker. In addition to answering the phone and taking down messages, I eventually learned to clerk auctions, listening to the fast-moving ramble and writing down the number of the person who bought each lot, and the sale amount, so they could pay at the end. It was one of my favorite ways to spend a Saturday. Pipe and cigarette smoke floated on the outside air, and lunchtime meant a hot dog from the food truck before food trucks were cool. My parents and Uncle Addison praised my ability to work, to clerk, and to answer phones. It made me proud to be good at something, and I worked even harder.

Our life had a set routine and structure. Every Sunday morning, Sunday night, and Wednesday night, we attended the neighborhood church, only two blocks from our house. The white-haired, white-bearded pastor looked like my idea of God, with his booming voice and Broadway stage presence.

Since my mother was busy with schoolwork and the real estate business, she hired me as the maid for five dollars a week, and I cleaned the house every Friday after school. Her main domestic provision was to provide supper Monday through Friday, food on the table at 4:40 p.m. when my dad got home from his state job. The early supper left time for showing houses or making phone calls in the evenings.

Food was never given a lot of thought, and her usual repertoire included a frozen entrée, mashed potatoes from dehydrated potato flakes, and vegetables from a can. She said she had to cook all those years for farmhands with her mother, and she was tired of it. The truth is, she was never wired for domestic chores. Even now, when we visit my mother every Sunday after church, she feeds us soup made with ketchup and roast that is dried out on the edges.

Her mission was to take care of a basic need so things of importance could be done. My experience in Italy seems to be the opposite. The focus on fresh ingredients, the fellowship time when friends and family can sit around the table and face each other—these seem to indicate the meal *is* the thing of importance.

∽

I push thoughts of Italy out of my mind and try to focus on the monthly financial reports for my gift shop, spread out on the table: a balance sheet, profit and loss, and year-to-year comparison. In one brief semester of college madness, I thought I wanted to pursue business as a degree, so I took accounting and received a generous C for my efforts. I never understood the basic concept of debits and credits and always got them the wrong way around. The misery ended when I switched to communications the following semester, but now here I am, wishing I had a better grasp of accounting principles after starting two businesses.

I pour another cup of coffee, stare out the window to give my eyes a break, and find myself reflecting on the reasons I started a soap shop and guesthouses. For the shop, it was to create an experience for customers to buy handcrafted regional items, including our own small-batch goat milk soap and bath products, to support local farmers and artisans, and to provide quality gifts and everyday consumables. For the guesthouses, it was to create beautiful and comfortable spaces for travelers to stay and experience a small, rural town. A place to be refreshed and rejuvenated. Creation is at the core of both, and so are hospitality and hopes to provide our guests and customers a little sense of renewal when they stop in and visit, an opportunity for peace and calm.

Peace and calm are the very elements I am missing with the burden of technology issues, managing people, inventory, accounting reports, and marketing, duties that need to be done by competent people. I find myself spending all my time doing tasks I have little natural aptitude for, while my own gifts shrivel in the sun.

I am facing a similar issue with my writing. More than a year has passed since our two weeks in Italy, and my second book is now ready to launch, meaning the creative process is over and now we are down to the business of marketing and events. It's a celebratory time, but there are so many things to do and so little time to do them.

My gaze turns to the stack of dishes that arrived last November from Italy, the dishes I bought from Francesca's art and ceramic studio. Another November has rolled around, and Benedetta will have her lemon trees safely tucked into the *limonaia* for the winter. Francesca will be busy painting ceramics for all the summer orders that now must be fired and shipped. We made a short trip back this last summer with our family, but it wasn't enough, only a taste of something delicious that couldn't be fully consumed.

Pruning is in the back of my mind, but I see no immediate solution other than shutting down the businesses, and I don't want to do that. I drain the last drop of coffee from my mug, gather the financial reports and toss them in the trash. My mother is waiting on me to take her out to lunch.

"Are you leaving me now?" she says, when I reach for my purse and stand to go after our lunch outing. Guilt rushes in like dirty water backing up in a clogged sink. I am eager to go home, but this woman who raised me to work, to be independent, and modeled it vociferously herself when I was a child, is now needy for me.

I sit back down and feel a migraine coming on.

"I guess I can drink another cup of coffee." I stay another thirty minutes, which placates her.

On the way home, I think about my upcoming birthday, when I will turn fifty. I remember my father warning me that "turning fifty is hard on a man" when Jess approached his fiftieth birthday a few years back. I reckon turning fifty can be just as hard on a woman, but maybe it can also be a new start.

I intend to look at my fiftieth birthday as a stake in the ground for a change, to set new goals for a new and improved life—a life that allows my gifts to flourish and trims away the life-draining vines, giving way for new growth.

Things will be different when I turn fifty, I promise myself.

CHAPTER

N⅀ 6

O ver the years, I have learned that I am the sole planner in the family and if anything is to happen, it's up to me to plan the parties—and that includes my own birthday celebrations. After a few times of sitting around and waiting for a party that never happens, you figure out it's worth it to do it yourself. If birthdays mean anything to you, that is, and for me, they are important milestones worthy of marking.

I have left nothing to chance for this important celebration. There will be a trip to the sea with our best friends and traveling buddies, Wes and Roni Perry, for a week of soaking up the sun, splashing in the ocean, and eating seafood. When we return home, I am hosting our family for a birthday party where everyone must dress as their favorite literary character. We have been planning our outfits for weeks, and the kids are just as excited as the adults.

First, our trip to the sea with our dear friends. Wes and Roni are from Midland, Texas. They are both fit and athletic, kind and warm, generous and loving. Jess and Wes always spend long hours talking business when they are together, while Roni and I share our souls in deep personal talks. Roni and I both have introverted natures, so we give each other the freedom to have time alone and then enjoy our time together. That's what has made our couple friendship work so well over the years. Hearty belly laughs are abundantly peppered through our time together, but faith is at the core of our friendship, beginning from our first meeting many years ago on a Young Life committee for the Dominican Republic and extending to trips around the world together.

We are enjoying our time when, just a couple of days into the trip, on the eve of my birthday, a call comes through: There's been a tragic accident at home. We scramble to throw clothes into suitcases, change flights, and say tearful goodbyes to our friends.

Instead of a birthday celebration on the beach, Jess and I are sitting next to his dad's hospital bed in the critical care unit of the University of Kentucky Medical Center. His eighty-eight-year-old father suffered an accidental gunshot wound.

For six weeks, we drive back and forth from Stanford to Lexington, taking turns staying with him in a rotation of other family members, hoping and praying for a miracle. We get good news, then bad news, then good news; it's a corkscrew of emotion. We are all amazed at his strength as he fights through four surgeries and the extended care, but six weeks after the accident, he dies on our daughter Adrienne's birthday. It is the same day she held her husband's memorial service three years before.

I thought I was tired before this happened, but now the weariness is beyond words. My journal gathers dust. Jess's usually exuberant voice is subdued. He is dealing with not only the loss of his father but also the loss of his primary business mentor and life guide. He is now thrust into the role of taking over his father's business decisions, and his grief is multilayered.

Grief, like interest, compounds. I find I am grieving my father-in-law and all the deaths leading up to his. The deaths have come like angry waves in recent years, and we are barely able to recover from one before another wave hits. The first tidal wave of grief began with the death of my father eight years before, followed weeks later by Jess's mother, then four more aunts and uncles gone within six months.

The year after that, an exchange student drowned in my father-in-law's swimming pool, followed the next year by the death of my childhood best friend from an aggressive cancer, and two years after that, our son-in-law, also to cancer. Sorrow upon sorrow.

I long for the old days when those grieving could wear black for a year, or at least six months, as a way of saying, "I'm not quite right yet. A little extra kindness, please." But there's no outward sign available today, nothing to invite an extra portion of grace.

After going through the grieving process so many times recently, I've figured out that people give you about two weeks to get back in the saddle, especially if you've already been out taking care of someone with an extended illness. Life comes rushing back at you, and commitments made before a tragedy still must be kept.

Such are my thoughts as I think about a speech I agreed to do a year ago to 200 business people. It's been only a few short months since this latest tragedy, and I am still not quite right.

Why am I doing this and how did I get here? Sometimes I say yes to a commitment because I want to do the thing. Sometimes I say yes because I know the thing will be good for me, possibly stretch me. Far too often, I say yes simply to please somebody, or many bodies, because I think it is something I should do.

Maybe it was a little of all three, but now I am regretting the decision.

The topic is vague at best, and the countless hours I have spent trying to figure out what in the world to say are mind-boggling. Even worse, I am supposed to speak on this nebulous topic for twenty minutes. I resolve this will be the last of my vague speeches, part of the deadwood I am eager to snip. In the meantime, I am left to fulfill obligations made before I became so enlightened.

For a little added pressure, it's the home county of my mother's side of the family, so the Huletts will be there in force, hoping to be proud of one of their own. My mother will sit like a queen at the front table in her rhinestone-studded vest, wearing more glitter than Dolly Parton, receiving congratulations for her ability to birth such a wonder child. Or so she hopes it will go.

I am furiously practicing my speech in front of a tree near the back porch when a phone call comes through. A vitriolic disagreement between employees at the soap shop has resulted in a walkout of our production staff—one longtime employee and two part-time ladies. It's been simmering for a while, and now the volcano erupts at the worst possible time. I sit down on the porch steps and feel as if I might throw up.

Three hours later, I deliver my speech while my mother sparkles her pleasure to all her friends and family. I sit down and feel a sense of relief, followed by a sense of foreboding.

Tomorrow I have to go back to work in the store. We create our bath products in the basement of the retail shop, but that space will sit empty and lifeless without a team to do the work. I am the only one left who knows how to make our products; the rest of the staff are new and unfamiliar with the process and will be needed to keep the doors open for our customers.

How did I get here? The same question haunts me again. I feel deeply hurt and betrayed, yet I've always heard the fish rots from the head. I am, unfortunately, the head. What did I do wrong?

∽

The soapmaking and product mixing is hard, physical work. After four solid weeks of daily work, a ten-pound weight loss, and an acne breakout that rivals my teenage years, I finally have relief in sight with the return of one of the former production workers.

I climb the steps to the cream hopper and heft the five-gallon bucket of mixed lotion to the top, where it slides like custard into the opening. I scrape

the bucket and then climb back down before cranking up the pumping machine. As the rhythmic and hypnotic work of pumping the body cream into jars begins, my thoughts drift to Tuscany and a sunny sabbatical. The word *sabbatical* comes to me like a sweet fragrance, or maybe it's just the lavender essential oil that now permeates the air. I take a deep breath, hoping it will deliver on the promise to relax.

⁓

Even though the physical work is over, a fatal blow has been struck to my confidence. The soap shop and the guesthouses are like two children for me. But as with children, I am being forced to acknowledge that they have grown beyond what I can offer. I am a maker, a starter, a dreamer. I am not a manager. My strength is to create and give life, but now they need a different kind of guidance.

These children won't leave me for college or for marriage, forcing a break and a new chapter. They will stay right under my thumb as long as I want to keep my thumb pressed down on them. I have to be the one to let go. If I don't, the businesses, and more importantly the people inside the businesses, will not grow. I'm stunting myself, too, if I spend all my energy trying to wrangle with something beyond my gifts.

A truth forms in my mind and takes solid shape. It's been there for a while now, but I've been too close to see it. It's time to step away and let someone else take it from here. Someone who can take the businesses to the next level. I don't know how or when, but it must happen.

⁓

I begin to cling with hope to a word, one that keeps being mentioned around me by my pastor, by a friend in academics, in a book I am reading: *sabbatical.* I roll the word around in my mouth, the very name of it eliciting thoughts of sabbath rest. Those thoughts grow in my mind, and so does the longing for something like that myself. Time apart to read, study, and rest.

Annual but short summer trips to Montefollonico are welcome reprieves but leave me wanting more of what we experienced on the first trip: the intense creativity, the full experience of each moment, the fresh perspective. It's as if I have tasted what *could be* and now there is a restlessness under the yoke of *what is*.

Sabbatical means longer than two weeks. It's an extended period of time to pull away, to disengage, and to listen to the still, small voice of God. The white noise is so loud in my day-to-day life that I can hardly hear anything. I long for the communion I feel when I am still and silent in nature, reading verses that speak deeply to my heart, feeling my very soul quiet in a way that opens me up to receive God's love and grace. I am desperate for that. What if we had a place of our own in Italy—some small refuge where we could put our own sheets on the bed and leave clothes that would be waiting for us when we returned again? What if?

My longing for sabbatical transfers to a longing for Italy. My mind often goes back to those sunny days spent in that charming Tuscan village the last few summers, reliving a meal, or a morning hike through the trees, or a lingering view of Monte Amiata over a foamy cappuccino.

An icy winter wind snaps me back into reality on this New Year's Day, and despite the chill, a sense of hope for second chances and new starts warms me with anticipation. It's our day to review our plans and goals for the year as a couple, a tradition we started the first year we were married. I am contracted to write a third novel this year, and I want to go on another trip to Italy, since I plan on wrapping up my trilogy by throwing my main character an Italian wedding.

"The literacy center in Lexington is offering a beginner's Italian class on Monday nights," I tell Jess. "The beginner class is six weeks, and then they offer another level after. We could try the first class and see if we like it."

"When is it?"

"Monday nights."

"All the way downtown?"

"It starts at five thirty, so we can go to dinner afterward. It could be fun."

Jess squirms. I know he doesn't love the thought of an hour's drive to Lexington at the end of a workday. Not only that, but he is far more comfortable in a boardroom than a classroom. He dropped out of college in his third year and never looked back.

"We're in a rut. We need to push ourselves outside our comfort zone and do something interesting, like we do when we're in Italy. Learning is good for the brain, and we can try out some different restaurants for dinner in Lexington afterward."

"I guess so."

"We don't have to do part two if we don't like it. I'll only sign up for part one." My husband's agreement is tacit at best, but I check that line off my agenda and move on. "Remember when we were in Montefollonico last summer and we visited the Italians who had a small summer apartment in the old convent? I was thinking, maybe we could look into something like that. A small place to stay when we visit. After all, we've been to Montefollonico for three years in a row, and we don't seem to want to go anywhere else. Maybe we can look around when we go this year."

"Hmm. It would probably be a good idea to see it in a different time of year, make sure we like another season, maybe the spring."

When dating someone, you want to see them in all kinds of situations before you take the plunge. Montefollonico in spring, I realize, might be very different than the bustling month of August. It's a good idea.

"But better call Howard before we get too far down the road," he cautions.

Howard Dayton is our spiritual mentor and financial counselor. His counsel has been invaluable over the years, and the studies he created on how to handle money with biblical principles have transformed not only Jess and me but also our family members and our businesses. Howard knows what Italy means to me, and he has long known of my struggle as an introvert being married to an extrovert. He appreciates the need to stop and refill the well after a season of giving out to others because he has experienced it himself.

"I'll call him," I offer. If I leave the task to Jess, he might get around to it in the next month. I feel a sense of urgency. If this idea is dead on arrival, I need to know now so I can stop dreaming.

I call Howard the next day. When he answers, I lay out the idea of purchasing a small property in Montefollonico and then hold my breath.

"I would be cautious if it seems to complicate your life in any way," Howard says. He recently lost his wife, Bev, to breast cancer. He is going through his own season of scaling down, cleaning out his house, distributing items to his children, and keeping only the things he needs. Simplicity is in the forefront of his mind. "But I think it's fine to take the next step."

Maybe I am justifying it, but a place of our own in this village we have come to love is a *reason* to simplify every other area of our life. We have been talking for two years about how to move me out of the day-to-day operations with our downtown hospitality businesses, and still there have been no major changes. Having a place in Italy to write, to be creative, to let possibilities fly and fully be who God created me to be, could sustain me until that solution can be found. And when we're not there, it could be a place to share with others rather than something kept all to ourselves.

At the same time, we've always resisted the idea of a second home. It does seem like a complication to keep up with two households, and a second home tends to tie you down to a certain place. We've never seriously considered it before. But somehow, it feels different this time.

I book Francesca's apartment for May and initiate a connection with an Umbrian pastor not far from Montefollonico, whom we hope to meet while we are there. If we are exploring the idea of establishing roots, we want to know fellow believers in the area, another step toward creating a home away from home.

CHAPTER
No 7

Jess breaks a tooth within hours of our arrival in Italy. I am slightly shocked that teeth actually break in Italy, that anything so mundane can happen in such a place as this, but apparently, we are still this side of paradise. Francesca directs us to a dentist in a nearby town who speaks English. The empty waiting room is modern and minimalist, a bit sterile, but an American flag is hanging in the entrance foyer as a welcome.

The dentist is kind and personable, his English far better than our Italian, even after we took both Italian part one and part two in Lexington. He makes a small repair that will suffice for the next few weeks, until Jess can return home for a more extensive fix.

Crisis averted, we settle into Francesca's rental apartment, which feels comfortably familiar by now. We are eager to practice our newly learned, albeit basic, Italian. We enjoyed our classroom time so much that we extended from six weeks to twelve and had a four-course Italian dinner together with our classmates at the end to celebrate. We officially know how to conjugate five verbs in present tense.

We take a walk around the village, and I find I can almost

read the notices posted along our route. One flyer advertises a Mother's Day luncheon hosted by one of two cooking schools that call Montefollonico home. The deadline to sign up has passed, but I make a beeline for the market, *alimentari*, in case there is room for one more.

The three ladies who run the market are also the backbone of the parish, making them doubly in the center of Montefollonico. Giuseppina is the mother and can usually be found behind the deli counter slicing cheese and cured meats. She is lovely and smiling, with a kind and gentle spirit.

Isabella, the older daughter, emanates stability, dependability, and sensibility. She speaks a smattering of English, and she always seems to be learning more. Ilaria is the younger daughter, saucy and fun, with a hint of mischief in her eyes.

The doors slide open and Isabella turns from the cash register.

"*Ciao*, Angela!" No one is waiting in line, so she stands and gives me a kiss on both cheeks in greeting.

"*Isabella, la festa di mamma, pranzo?*" The Mother's Day lunch, I am trying to say.

"*Sì.*" She waits, smiling, knowing I am trying to learn her language.

"*Okay per me . . .*" I struggle for the Italian version of "to go" but can't find it.

"*Sì, chiamo. Aspetta.*"

She will call. I am supposed to wait. She returns to tell me it is fine, that I am welcome to come.

I feel slightly bad about leaving Jess on a Sunday afternoon to eat on his own just as we have arrived.

"Go! Have fun! I'll be fine," he says.

The luncheon is held in the *Teatro di Montefollonico*, a part-time theater and part-time community center. This is my first time inside the theater, and I enter a small foyer where I buy my ticket. Then there is a big, open room with maroon seats pushed to the side to make space for long tables and chairs set up on the terra-cotta floor. An elevated stage at one end is framed by thick velvet curtains.

The walls are blush and the trim is a deeper shade of rose. We are seated at the communal tables, and three courses are brought by men who have volunteered to be the servers.

I am placed next to some English speakers and meet an American named Sally, the only American I have met in the village. We exchange information, and I tell her we are thinking of buying a small apartment in the village. She offers to show us their home and share their experiences of buying real estate in Italy.

Getting advice from Sally seems to be another step toward the dream becoming a reality, but before I can pump her with more questions, a bustling takes place up front on the stage. It appears, to my delight, we are in for a show. The crowd is hushed, and we turn our chairs to see the production.

I've witnessed the Italian flair for dramatics through exchanges as a tourist, but as it now plays out on stage, I am not disappointed. The village women act out vignettes that both honor and make fun of all the things mothers—or simply women—must handle. The Italian ladies around me laugh uproariously. I clap as if I understand every word, which I don't, but I find it doesn't matter. Today, we are all women, sisters, daughters, and mothers, no matter the cultural differences.

◇◇◇

While this trip is an exploration of Montefollonico in another season, and a possible look into owning property here, it is also meant to provide me with another two weeks to make progress on the final book in the trilogy. I have a looming deadline, but considering the ease with which I wrote so much of the second book in our first two weeks here, I have high hopes that Italy will work its magic for me again.

On Monday morning, I open my laptop, wait for inspiration, and spend most of the time staring at the wall. I change writing spots in hopes that will help. It doesn't. Jess sends an email to the real estate agent inquiring about a viewing for two available apartments in the restored convent at the top of the hill outside Montefollonico. We go out for lunch, and then I make a second attempt after a stiff cup of coffee to counter the pasta.

I tap a few sentences, stare at the screen, and look out the window. Unlike before, when the words flowed like milk, this time feels like pouring sorghum in winter. I am writing about Thanksgiving and a Christmas wedding in the middle of May, with birds chirping outside and a beckoning breeze that calls to me, "Come take a walk."

I let out a deep sigh and decide I've struggled enough for one day. Tomorrow, I will get up even earlier and tackle it again. The break helps, and when I return to my writing station the next morning, after an hour or so of wrestling again, I zero in on the problem. A headstrong character is supposed to show up in a climactic scene, but every time I write the scene, it falls flat. I write and rewrite, then whine to Jess, hoping he will tell me it's okay to give it up for now and simply enjoy being in Italy. He doesn't, so I keep circling around the problematic scene, moving instead to other parts of the book until I can legitimately walk away from this uncooperative character at the respectable hour of noon.

Jess receives confirmation for an appointment that afternoon to see the convent apartments. I feel as if I am about to go on a first date with someone who promises to be the man of my dreams. It's a welcome distraction from writer's block.

The convent grounds are well landscaped with shady trees and slender cypresses. The caretaker shows us the common spaces, including the monks' dining area, which now serves as a museum of sorts for the convent's history, and the chapel that is available for residents to reserve.

We walk to the apartments down dimly lit halls that seem to require hushed tones. When Jess asks a question and his voice ricochets around the hallway, I cringe as if we might wake the dead. The caretaker jingles keys as he opens the door to the apartment that is actually in our price range. I remind myself to breathe through the anticipation.

One room offers space for a couch and a kitchen with a small table. We climb ladderlike stairs to a loft where there is a bedroom, and then two steps down to a bathroom. I imagine waking in the middle of the night, tripping down the steps or pitching headfirst over the loft railing. Though a small window offers a picturesque view of the gardens and the countryside in the distance, the space feels stifling.

We leave that apartment and twist and turn down hallways to another one, far out of our price range but worth seeing as a comparison. While we access it from the same sparse hallway, we enter into a generous room with high ceilings and a fireplace that holds great promise. This positive first impression is diminished when we see that the rest of the apartment is accessed by climbing

down a hole here and up a small ladder there, with bathrooms tucked into nooks and crannies, much like a small ship.

Jess turns back to the caretaker and asks, "Any other apartments for sale?"

"Only these two."

The door clicks shut on the last apartment, and we make a beeline through the stark and cavernous hallway to the outside door and breathe in gulps of sunshine. Jess is tight-lipped, but he manages a smile for the caretaker, thanks him, and gives him a tip for his trouble. We dart off the convent grounds like prisoners on the run.

"It felt so . . . monastic!" I shudder.

"It is a monastery."

"Convent, but what's the difference?"

It's been my long-held opinion that houses speak and walls talk. Not in a verbal sense, but in a quiet, whisper-on-the-wind way. It's a feeling, a sense of time beyond the present, and sometimes a recognition of good and evil. Maybe there was great dissent among the inhabitants that embedded itself in the very timbers and trusses. Or possibly some unspeakable trauma was hidden and squashed, until it pushed itself into the walls. Sometimes a house emanates joy and warmth from souls that lived loving and generous lives.

But the convent felt lifeless, perhaps owing to the part-time nature of many of the residents, or maybe it was the access to these two apartments—echoing halls that contrasted with the charming apartment we previously viewed off the sunny gardens. Either way, I did not sense a whisper of "home" for us.

We stop by to see Francesca and ask if she knows of any local properties available for sale. "There is one particular house. If you like, I will call the owner. She lives in Siena, but I think there is a neighbor who has a key."

This house is just outside the village wall. The caretaker speaks no English at all, but he smiles, unlocks the door, and waits for us to make the rounds.

It has a sweet feel to it, as if it might be owned by an aunt who loves to stuff you full of comforting, creamy pasta.

There is a room with outside access that needs renovation and a dark cantina. There is a delightfully tree-shaded yard that, with some work, could be beautiful. The view is limited, though, and after becoming used to seeing Monte Amiata from Francesca's garden, we struggle with the thought of losing that lovely vista. It is half the price of the small convent apartment, which is a decided plus. We thank the neighbor and hike back up the hill to our apartment.

"I liked it."

"It has potential," Jess agrees.

We are silent the rest of the walk home.

∽

While I am distracted by the village activity and fight-writing with this irascible character, Jess has set up his studio for painting in the extra bedroom. He rounded up the paints, brushes, and small canvases on his own this time, without me secreting them away.

The upstairs bedroom window looks out on the street, and it provides excellent light. Sometimes I sneak up the stairs and linger for a few minutes, watching him paint from beyond the door. He studies the scene outside before touching brush to canvas, and for an hour or two, he is lost to a world of color and beauty.

His work in Italy seems even more inspired with vibrancy, and a dance of light and shadow that is just right. He senses it, too, and is drawn to his studio more than before.

One evening, Jess is upstairs painting and I am soaking in the tub, staring out the open bathroom window to the sky above when, like Archimedes's own bathtub experience, revelation hits me. I don't cry "Eureka!" and run naked in the streets, but I do rise out of the tub with such force that water laps over the edge. I grab a towel and climb awkwardly over the high edge, then run, dripping, into the living area. I settle onto the couch and open my laptop, eager to revise my manuscript.

This character that I have been forcing into a scene has been an absentee father to my main character during the first two books. That's what he's been trying to tell me. Why would he show up now for an important event when he's always failed his daughter? It's completely contrary to his normal behavior. I rewrite some key sections and begin to feel the warm satisfaction of a good writing flow that has eluded me on this trip until now. The house hunt may be stalled, but the book is back on track.

⁓

The young Umbrian pastor we connected with before leaving has invited us to dinner in Perugia. Giacomo Sardone and his wife, Miriam, live in a small apartment complex on the edge of the city, and we find it without any trouble. Giacomo is only thirty years old, newly married to Miriam, who is even younger, and they both look as if they could be on the Italian movie screen. They have invited some of the elders of the church—all young people, so the word *elders* doesn't seem quite right—over for dinner as well. They are a mature group of believers, serious about following Christ and showing their love for the city of Perugia.

Seated at the Sardones' table, we find out that Giacomo studied wine before he followed the call to become a pastor, like his father before him. He is from Siena, where his father is currently still pastoring. Miriam works as a physical therapist but also sings on the worship team. The dinner discussion ranges from ministry to wine to the history of Perugia.

We enjoy a fellowship transcending age, language, and culture. As the evening wraps up, we take pictures together, bid goodnight, and drive back to Montefollonico, having no idea how significant this meeting and this family will become to us in the future.

CHAPTER
№ 8

hough August afternoons push us inside to rest from the heat, we have discovered spring afternoons are perfect for a long walk in the *parco* that connects to the village. Nearly two hundred years ago, the Landucci family, one of the three noble families in Montefollonico, decided to donate a hundred acres of land to the village to use as a public park with hiking trails. It is used often by the locals and it's a necessary part of our day, balancing our tendency to indulge in pasta, bread, and wine.

People aren't the only trail users. The wild boar, or *cinghiale*, root around the side of the trails. Evidence of their presence is everywhere on the sides of the mountain paths where rooted dirt is upturned. I am sometimes wary, hoping we will not surprise one on the trail.

Broom bush offers a fragrant scent as we pass by and is distinctive not only for the yellow flower but also the long spindly sticks that have traditionally been used to make brooms. Through the trees, we catch occasional glimpses of fields where red poppies and wildflowers sprinkle the meadows. I try not to tread on the tiny purple flowers dotting the soft grass next to the trail. Tuscany in the springtime is full of blooming colors that seem to rise wild in the meadows and on the mountain paths. The scent is fresh and floral, and the warmth of the sun counters the cool wind that still reminds us that summer has not yet arrived.

We are climbing a steep path and Jess offers his hand, steadying me until we reach the top. As we pause to gaze at the view, an idea comes to me.

"Remember when I was single and wrote down my list?"

"Your nonnegotiables." He's heard me tell the story often, and we've shared it with countless single friends. One broken relationship after another inspired me to write a list of nonnegotiables for any future suitors.

If it works for business contracts, why not for a spouse? I thought back then, comparing it to my work as a meeting planner. I decided that my future husband must love and honor God, act with integrity, have a sense of adventure along with a sense of humor—and that we had to have chemistry. Jess had all those attributes and many more I never thought to list.

"Maybe we need a list of nonnegotiables for this property search. That way, we're protected from choosing something that doesn't really align with our truest desires. One of mine is a house inside the village. After spending that vacation with our family at the bottom of the hill, I realized the value of an easy walk to the market and to restaurants. What about you?"

Jess opens his arms to the rolling hills in front of us. "A view is on my list."

"Does it matter which view?" With a town that rides the ridge between the Val d'Orcia and the Val di Chiana, the views are vastly different.

"No, either one," he says without hesitation.

"Anything else?"

"I do not want a renovation."

"Agreed." I heartily endorse this comment. In the last several years, we have renovated seven houses and several commercial spaces in 100- to 200-year-old buildings. It's part of why I am here, to get away from all that. I am not interested in tackling ancient dust and rubble. Italy is our place of rest from work and the businesses.

"I wouldn't mind if there was something to do in the future, but nothing that keeps us from staying in the house immediately," he adds.

"Sure, a future remodel might be fun, but we must be able to move in right away. Inside the village, with a view, and no renovation. We have our list."

⌀

Jess has been tenacious about searching the internet for available properties, but nothing has surfaced. We are two days from going home, and it doesn't appear that this trip will offer up anything in the form of a viable prospect. Despite this, my writing has gone well, and the first draft is nearly finished. My agent will be happy, our Italian is better, we are rested, and we've reconnected with old friends. We even leave this time with new friends, Giacomo and Miriam. We have taken a step deeper into the community, but we haven't found a house.

I begin to gather our belongings, scattered here and there all over the apartment, when I'm startled by a yell from the next room.

"Ang, you're not gonna believe this."

"What?" I race to the room, alarmed.

"I was typing in the wrong town this whole time. It has to be Torrita di Siena, since that's the official seat of business for Montefollonico. There's a bunch in the area," he says.

"Where?"

"In the village, outside the village. I'll go through them and then we can look at the best ones."

An hour later, we are sitting in front of his iPad.

"This one is really interesting," he says. "It's just up the street. We've walked by it a hundred times."

I lean over his shoulder and look at the pictures. It doesn't look familiar to me, even though I must have passed right by it many times. "Can we see it?"

"I'll email them. I like a couple more, but this is the most intriguing."

It is on our end of the village, looking off the other side of the mountain, and right next door to the restaurant where we first saw the view toward Cortona on *Ferragosto*—the view I said was the most beautiful I had ever seen, a view this house will share.

While waiting to hear back from the real estate agent, we lace up our shoes and walk into the street to check it out. I gaze up at the building; it is not particularly attractive from the outside. The walls are plastered, unlike the honey stone on the buildings to either side of it, and the plaster has aged to a grayish shade of ugly, or *brutto*, as the Italians would say. Brown shutters, circa 1970, cover the windows, but the one redeeming quality I can see

is a beautiful medieval-looking door in the center, flanked by two additional doors that open onto the street.

We take a walk in the *parco*, fueled partly by nervous energy, and by the time we return, there is an email from the agent. He can meet us this afternoon.

～◎∽

Leo is young and dashing, dressed in a black leather jacket, T-shirt, and jeans, as if he were about to go clubbing. We introduce ourselves and make small talk on the street while we wait for the caretaker to arrive with the key to the house. Leo rolls out papers with floor plans to show us.

The buzzing motor of an Ape gets our attention as it rounds the corner at the piazza. *Ape* means "bee" in Italian. It's not much more than a motorbike, but unlike the Vespa, whose name means "wasp," this stinger has three wheels, an enclosed cab, and a small truck bed in the back, which makes it an extremely useful vehicle in tiny medieval streets.

The Ape buzzes toward us and parks next to the house. The green metal hood is polished to a shine. An older gentleman steps out, and when he turns to face us, I catch my breath. The shape of his face, receding hairline, kind eyes, and stature all resemble my beloved, deceased uncle Addison. He was a dear uncle to me, the one who helped my parents get a start in the real estate business. I remember him sharing the Smarties he kept in his office desk drawer, taking us on vacations to Florida, and guiding my father in business. We even shared our birthday celebrations, March 10 and 11. He was a well-known auctioneer, handsome, divorced from his first wife and on his second marriage to a fun-loving woman with a cackling laugh. Frequent weekend trips with them provided a lot of fun and laughter in my early years.

～◎∽

I am fighting everything I have not to embrace this Italian man, but I restrain myself and give him a simple handshake.

79

"His name is Alfonso," Leo says. *Alfonso*, I muse. Alfonso and Addison both start with an "A" and have three syllables and seven letters.

I watch as Alfonso takes out a jangling set of keys and unlocks the door. A tingling sensation runs up my spine, and I have a sense that when I step over this threshold, life will somehow change.

"The house was a horse stable," Leo tells us. "For the Mucciarelli Palazzo here." He points to the grand house or "palace" across the small street, a hulking structure that dwarfs the narrow *strada*. "The downstairs was used for stables and then as wine storage, with an apartment upstairs."

We step through that massive medieval-style doorway, and it takes a moment for my eyes to adjust to the diminished light. To our left is a cluttered office with stacks of dusty newspapers and magazines. A door on the right leads us into a garage filled with wooden ladders, gardening tools, brooms, pots, and even a bird cage.

High on the walls are terra-cotta medallions. One dates the most recent renovation of the barn to 1892. The shape of a horse head is cast into the clay of some, while others display a coat of arms or sunflowers. There are marble stones affixed to the wall as memorials to trotters, stating their noble characteristics along with the birth and death date of the horse being memorialized.

Jess and I look at each other, smiling. We are from Kentucky, the horse capital of the world, known for the Kentucky Derby. We've been around and on horses all our lives. Seeing the horse portraits on the terra-cotta medallions makes the space feel unexpectedly like home.

The vaulted ceilings, also made of terra-cotta, are held by steel beams painted to match. Another door to the right leads into a long room with three giant concrete vats for wine. We can only imagine how this room might look with the hulking concrete removed.

We walk outside and can barely take in the neglected terrace for the mouth-dropping view. The day is sunny and clear, and it's possible to see forty or fifty miles in several directions. Leo points out Lake Trasimeno in one direction, Cortona directly in front of us, Arezzo to another side, and the towers of Siena in the distance on the far left. The terrace features some stones and a patch of grass, but also a great deal of concrete. There are climbing vines, blooming rose bushes by the dozen, and red geraniums. Lemon trees sit in pots on the patio, the bright yellow fruit contrasting against the green leaves.

"A fig tree," Jess says. He rushes to the railing of the terrace to look for ripe figs, but the fruit is still green. I don't know how many times I've nearly rocketed through the windshield when Jess slammed on the brakes at the sight of a roadside fig tree. To have one's own fig tree would be an unimaginable luxury.

"Come," Leo says. "I will show you another horse stall."

We walk down crumbling rock steps to the lower terrace. It's a small strip of land where the fig and plum trees are rooted at steep angles, but there is a wide enough space for a small table and chairs if one desired. The disturbing part is the fifteen-foot drop to the land below with no fence for protection. I'm careful to watch my footing lest I tumble headlong over the edge of the yard.

We walk about ten feet into a cave-like tunnel, which opens to a beautiful brick vaulted space; I immediately imagine cool candlelight dinners in the heat of the summer. The space has many possibilities, but I can't fathom keeping horses here and then bringing them up the crumbling steps. Maybe things looked different in 1892.

Outside the dark room, I pause for a moment in the tall grass to take in the panoramic view that seems even more breathtaking after emerging from the darkness. I feel a sting on my ankle and look down. Alfonso points to a weed and speaks in Italian. "Nettles," Leo translates. "You must be careful."

We reenter the house and go upstairs, following the chair lift that carried the former resident, Gaetana—who lived into her nineties—up to the second floor through two switchbacks. Alfonso unlocks another door at the top of the steps. We step inside the apartment, still fully furnished and looking as if someone recently walked out to go to the market. One room has a tea table and two chairs, along with softer chairs placed for cozy chats with visitors. Another served as Gaetana's bedroom and contains a wardrobe and dresser. The bed is made up, a few personal items still sit on the dresser, and photographs of the Alps hang on the walls.

The only bathroom is in the hall, and across from it sits another smaller bedroom with two wardrobes and a daybed, apparently utilized as a dressing room.

The kitchen is empty, with new tile covering the walls. There are two more rooms at the back of the house, with windows that provide an expansive view of the valley floor below.

I cannot ignore a growing sense of familiarity with this house. It's as if the house is bursting with silent speech: *There you are! I've been waiting.*

Does Jess feel it too? Or am I creating a connection that is pure fantasy? We are with Leo and Alfonso, so we can only pass each other in the hall and make eye contact. His eyes are wide with excitement, and he raises his eyebrows as if to say, "This could be it." *He feels it too!* It is not my imagination.

IN MEMORIA

DELL' AFRICANA

FAMO   AVALLA

BUONA BRAVA B   EGANTISSIMA

DI GIUS. MUCCIARELL E SUA FAMIGLIA

FEDELE COMPAGNA DI VIAGGIO

PER BEN TRENT'ANNI

NATA A GROSSETO NEL 1872

MORTA IL 16 FEBBRAIO 1910

ALLA RARISSIMA ETÀ DI ANNI 38

Jess pauses before we leave the property and puts a hand on Alfonso's shoulder, but because of the language barrier, he directs a question to Leo.

"If we buy the house, does he go with it?" Leo translates into Italian for Alfonso. A chuckle, and then an answer.

"*Finche' potro' farlo.*" As long as I am able.

I hope he is able for a very long time.

I feel breathless when we walk out. Across the street a cat crouches next to the building. He has a tiny snake in his possession, and he watches us warily, as if we might take it from him. I have just had a heavenly experience, and it seems odd to see a dead snake, as if there is no way such a thing can belong in the world from which I have just emerged.

We say *arrivederci* and *grazie* to Leo, and I resist the urge to hug Alfonso, this sweet contact making me feel as if I had a mystical visit with my uncle.

We leave the house with the euphoria of a first date when everything clicks. That evening, we go through our checklist.

View, check.

Village, check.

Habitable, check. After all, someone had been living there until recently. Exceeding our checklist is its location at "our" end of the village—and a view that far surpasses anything we could have imagined.

∞

That night, I can't sleep. I am kept awake from the excitement of seeing the house and meeting Alfonso, but also the stinging pain in my ankle from the nettle. I wonder what the Italian word is for nettle and if, perhaps, they have named a motorbike after it.

Jess calls Leo the next morning and asks if we can view the house again. I finish writing the last line in my third novel and close my laptop with tears in my eyes after a satisfying wedding scene. I have come to know and love these characters as if they were my own family. I also sense it is time for us to part for a while. I need to send them out into the world with my full blessing while I step into a different season of life.

Instead of writing about adventures and family mysteries, I need to more fully live my own adventure and explore my own family mysteries for a time.

I also feel a small sense of urgency. I am afraid that if I don't make a change now and move on to something else, I'll be writing about these characters until I take my last breath. It is a comfortable place for me, but if I don't push myself out, I will miss the growth that comes with tackling something new.

For now, I am satisfied that I'll be seeing the characters many more times in rounds of rewrites, edits, and proofreading before they find their way into a reader's hands. Someday, God willing, we will come back together for a new story.

On this second visit to the house, I bring my camera to capture each space, each detail, and each architectural feature for later study when we return home. On the terrace, I soak up that valley view and take a deep breath, squeezing each drop of beauty from this view, this village, this idea of life.

In all the houses we have viewed over the years, never have we heard a house speak to us so clearly. We couldn't have predicted that the building that finally spoke to us would be a nobleman's stable in a medieval hilltop village in Tuscany.

CHAPTER
№ 9

W̲e've been home from Italy only a week. The mail is finally sorted, our bodies are adjusted to the time change, and we are back up to full speed with the businesses.

It's Friday night, our usual date night, and I curl up on the porch sofa, the dog beside me. Not quite hot enough for the overhead fan, it's warm enough to sit in shorts while we watch the sun drop below the hills on the far side of the pasture. Jess hands me a glass of white wine and places his glass of red on the table in front of us.

While there appears to be only a coffee table between his chair and my sofa, I know the expanse contains much more than that. It's as big as a house, a house on the other side of the ocean. We have not spoken about the house since we returned over a week ago, which is an amazing display of restraint on my part.

I am trying to give Jess lots of room to process. I know that inside his mind, a pendulum is swinging back and forth, with all the pros and cons. For me, there are only positives. I am trying not to care too much, but never in my life have I walked into a place and simply known it was mine.

My fiftieth birthday year was awash in disappointments and loss. Perhaps this is the fresh start I need for this new decade, even if it is delayed by a year.

"Have you thought any more about the house?" I say, giving him enough time to settle into his chair.

"Sure," he says, and leaves it there, begging me to ask the next question.

"What are you thinking?" *Is he going to make me grovel?*

"I think it's a good deal, but we should talk to Howard. We're not talking about a lock-and-leave condo anymore. This is a house." With that simple statement, he waves the caution flag. I take a deep breath and throttle down the speed.

"Good idea." I remind myself that my new mantra of letting go may include this dream as well.

※

Howard and Jess talk every week at seven thirty on Saturday mornings, at a time I am usually tucked away in my upstairs writing nook. Today, I am motivated to eavesdrop on their conversation, or at least the part about the house. I slip behind an open door, positioning myself where I can hear the conversation without being seen.

Jess gives Howard all the facts, and they talk back and forth. My hopes rise when it sounds as if Howard is giving his approval, at least from Jess's end of the conversation. They end the call and I emerge from behind the door, nonchalant, as if I had just completed important business with the door hinges.

"Well, what did Howard say?"

"About what?"

I roll my eyes. "You know what."

"He thinks it's fine as long as it doesn't become a complication." Jess's voice is reserved, and I know he's by no means done pondering this thing.

※

Jess does ponder for a few more days. I am patient, knowing this is part of his decision-making process. He needs the time and space to do it, even if it means we risk losing the house to other buyers. If I cut this short, he'll only do it later, which will be even more stressful if we're in the middle of the buying process.

"I think we'll make an offer," he says one morning over coffee. He tells me the number he's planning on offering and my heart sinks.

"They'll never take that."

"We'll see."

Jess is the trader in this family, but I did grow up with dinner table discussions about interest rates, commissions, contracts, and closing. They will not accept this number.

Jess floats an even lower offer than we discussed with Leo, but Leo cautions against offending the owner and losing the negotiation. Jess reluctantly goes with the original offer amount, and then we are emailed a multipage document that we must both initial on every page, sign twice, and then email back.

We wait. I chew my lower lip in anticipation of the rejection. More days pass, then Leo finally tells us the owner has rejected the offer after no less than three meetings to discuss it.

Leo reminds us that the house is one-of-a-kind, unique in the village, with an incredible view. It's an unusual opportunity, we are told. The owners are taking a trip soon, and the opportunity might slip away.

My lower lip is in shreds, but Jess is steely-eyed and focused. He proposes another low offer, sweetens the deal with a quick closing and no contingencies, and then asks for all the furniture in the house.

A new offer means a new set of documents with new signatures and new initials on each page. After the documents are emailed, I try to settle into my traditional summer routine of weeding my garden, harvesting vegetables, and canning, but Jess has us both in turmoil as he bats around all sorts of questions and uncertainties. In fairness, despite the fact that he has bought and sold numerous pieces of property over his career, this is a foreign country. We've had no time to research "How to buy real estate in Italy," no time to examine the potential pitfalls, no time to gather wisdom from experienced people.

"Are we sure?" He asks me the question I've grown familiar with in our married life. It's not really a question. It's a statement—his statement—that he's not sure anymore.

"Yes," I say, with as much confidence as I can muster. This is unusual for me. I can't think of another time in our marriage that I didn't cave when I felt him going wobbly.

I quote a line from one of our favorite movies, *Out of Africa*: "At least we will have been somewhere."

He knows exactly what I mean. Karen says this to Bror at the beginning of the movie when she's convincing him to marry her and go to Kenya. Despite the fact that the decision ends up being disastrous on multiple levels, in the end, they had a memorable experience and it made great material for books and a movie.

We've been lots of places. I've traveled in forty-five states and several foreign countries, and Jess's list is as long as mine. That's quite a lot of places to have been, but I've never *lived* anywhere outside a sixty-mile radius in central Kentucky. My people came over the Appalachian Mountains with Daniel Boone in the late 1700s, settled in Kentucky, and have been here ever since. Hardly a soul in my family lives more than two hours away. If one does venture off for a short while, they usually find their way back to Kentucky, as if pulled home by a great magnet under the limestone. We are rooted to the land and to the people, yet my longing for an experience in another place is strong.

With all the recent losses and the accompanying awareness of the brevity of life, and especially hitting a landmark birthday myself, I am feeling this urgency even more. I want to experience another place, to learn another language, to absorb another culture while we are still healthy and able to enjoy it. If we don't do it now, will we ever?

Leo returns to us with a close counteroffer, an apartment full of grand-motherly furniture, and a ticking clock. The owners are packing up for summer vacation in the mountains and we must respond soon.

While the ticking clock is a known literary device, real estate agents are masters at using it too. Time is passing, each minute a step closer to losing the property. The owners might abandon the sale, another buyer might swoop in to steal the prize, or some unnamed obstacle might prevent the sale from going through.

We make a final counteroffer and wait. In the midst of this waiting, I pull into my mother's driveway next to her brick ranch house that she has occupied for nearly forty years. I turn off the car and check the email on my phone one last time so I can keep it out of sight while visiting with her.

"*Congratulazioni*, your offer has been accepted!" I stop breathing for a moment, hardly able to believe it. Sitting in my car, I call Jess because there is no way I can wait. Besides, the owners have one foot in the car, and they are about to leave for the mountains, according to Leo.

"It's all here. Are we good to go?"

Silence on the other end of the phone.

This is the moment I've feared all along—that we'll get to this point and not actually take the last step. I brace myself.

More silence, and then, "I reckon so."

I whoop with excitement and he laughs. After scrawling signatures with my forefinger on the phone, I sit in the car for a few minutes. It feels like a big, happy moment to soak in and enjoy. I want to savor it before I have to wipe the silly grin off and face my mother.

"What were you doing out there?" she asks when I walk in.

"Nothing. Just returning an email." I feel like a teenager caught out past curfew.

She looks at me sideways but I hold firm. I'm not ready to tell her yet. Not until it's a sure thing. It won't be good news for her, and it's better to wait until the sale is final.

CHAPTER
№ 10

I t is official, but our jubilation is now channeled into getting even more paperwork done since the original copies must all be mailed to Italy with elaborate wax seals. We are to inform Leo when the money is sent so they can keep the owner *tranquillo*. I thought he was supposed to be relaxing in the mountains, but apparently he is pulsing with anxiety until he hears from Leo.

The closing date is set for a couple of weeks before we arrive. We need a power of attorney to represent us at the closing. We consider who we might ask to do this important job and land on Francesca, since she has already been our landlord, friend, and confidante.

As things seem to be cruising toward the finish line of the August 11 closing date, a bombshell drops.

We find out that we must pay a value-added tax, a 22 percent charge that is placed on the sale of the property. It's a shocking increase to the good price Jess worked to negotiate. On top of finding out our cost is 22 percent higher, the euro has been climbing steadily since we agreed to buy the house, meaning even more cost. This purchase is growing more expensive by the day.

Jess paces around our house like a high-strung thoroughbred as he considers this new information. We are in dire need of some of that *tranquillo* on this side of the Atlantic too.

Expecting it to all come crashing down at this moment, I try to prepare myself, to adjust my heart from wanting this thing, or anything, too much. To my surprise and relief, we go forward.

Then a new problem. We are notified that the all-important power of attorney documents are lost. Tracking information shows they were delivered on August 1, but it is now August 7. We are four days from closing, and the documents are nowhere to be found. Leo takes the tracking information to the Italian postal service and acts as a truffle dog, sniffing out the lost documents.

The next day, on August 8, my mother's birthday, we are granted a gift in the form of a miracle. The postman finds the documents under the seat in his car.

Late on the evening of August 11, I receive pictures from Francesca of the meeting as the final contract is read aloud, word for word, as Italian law requires. I show them to Jess the next morning, and we toast with our coffee cups and text our thanks to Francesca for representing us.

Shortly after the closing, in the darkest part of the night when fears grow larger than reality, I imagine my youngest grandson tumbling down the terrace and falling over the fenceless edge of the medieval wall that drops fifteen feet into the garden below. I sit up in bed; my heart is racing.

This fear for my grandson is representative of a more general foreboding that haunts me when I remember a dead snake and nettles. What have we done? To buy a house on the other side of the world is insane.

How many morality tales have I read in which one decision leads down the road to destruction? In the light of day, I can't bring myself to confess any of this to Jess. I am afraid he will agree with me, and the adventure will stop.

There's the rub. I crave the adventure, and worry that, in middle age, if this one passes by, there may not be another. I am slightly terrified in a giddy sort of way. Isn't the very definition of adventure doing something bold or risky? If there isn't some risk, is it really an adventure?

I take deep breaths and lie back in bed, and pray the prayer I have prayed all along. *God, if this is not of you, block the path.*

Aside from my fears of some unknown undoing, there is also the niggling thought that I need to tell my mother now. I've been skulking around like a kid, hiding the fact that something huge is taking place in my life.

My mother raised me to be independent, yet my independence is also the thing she fears. When I was single and worked with people all over the United States, she was terrified I would marry someone and move off to California. To her great relief, my marriage at thirty-two was to someone who brought me full circle back to the farm, only ten minutes from the place of my birth, and twenty minutes from her. Just when she thought I was safely ensconced close to her, I find myself having to tell her what she has always feared: Her baby girl and primary caretaker won't always be here in Kentucky for her anymore.

For all her independence, my mother has a great number of fears—fears that I am constantly trying to manage for her. Nowadays, I'm required to send her our flight information so she can track us across the ocean. If she doesn't hear from me a couple of times a day during our travels, I'll get two or three texts in a row saying: "Are you all right????" The twenty-four-hour news cycle feeds her worries, and she imagines every possible travel trauma.

"Don't get thrown in prison!" she warns before I leave on a trip. I'm a law-abiding citizen, with the exception of a few speeding tickets, so I'm not sure why she worries most about me wasting away in a foreign jail. Terrorism, natural disasters, and riots are also on the list, but jail seems to be her greatest fear.

We are due to leave in only a few days to take ownership of a house we have purchased. I must tell her now. My sisters will know, word will get out, and the thing she hates most in the world is for someone to have information before her.

I've put it off because I don't know how to explain, to her or to any of my other family members, that we've bought a property in Montefollonico. It's strange for me to say we now have a home in Italy. A vacation house in Florida might be understandable, but not a house in a foreign country.

How will my mother ever comprehend this desire? What I can't explain to her is that Italy is also a mother to me, a mother who nurtures my creativity, my sense of community, adventure, and wonder. In an ironic twist, my mother is also an artist, a creative who gave me an Italian name, a stamp of predestination.

I don't know how to explain it, but I have to do the deed, and soon. We leave for Italy in a matter of days. We schedule lunch and I invite my older sister, Mom's firstborn, thinking this will help soften the blow.

My sister is already at my mother's house when I arrive, admiring my mother's latest piece of artwork.

Though Mom's early creative years were squashed by survival, she took up painting in her fifties when I went to college. She claimed her art was therapy, partly induced by the empty nest and partly her own need to express the pent-up creativity that had lain dormant while she worked for financial solvency.

Her first endeavor was painting toothpicks to look like pencils. Then there was the painted gourd stage, when she decided to grow and dry her own gourds for painting. Vines with gourds the size of basketballs covered the back patio, which became a bit of an artistic statement all its own.

From the gourds, she experimented with saw blades, rocks, pieces of wood, and eventually landed on boards and canvases, joining the conventional wisdom of artists worldwide.

Her best works are a series of folk paintings that speak of her idyllic childhood, carried by stores and purchased by clients from Kentucky to California, but she can't seem to stay in that more lucrative lane. A typical artist, she is always trying something new, and now she is into abstracts, a strange series of geometric shapes in various pinks, golds, and blues.

After the requisite tour and praise that is expected, we land at the kitchen table with hot mugs of coffee before going to lunch.

"Where's your next trip?" My sister asks, since she knows there's always one on the horizon. What a perfect segue.

"Italy, next week." I look down into my coffee to gather courage. "We just bought a house in the village we like."

A coffee cup thumps on the table and I feel my mother staring.

"Really? Are you moving there?" asks my sister.

"Not until after I die," Mom says. The stare is now a glare.

"No, we're not moving. A few weeks here and there, and then to share with our friends and family. I want you both to come. You'll love it!" I sound excessively enthusiastic even to my own ears.

I look at my mom to emphasize the invitation. She raises her eyebrows, rolls her eyes, and turns her head away. She is eighty-seven going on sixteen.

CHAPTER
N̲o̲ 11

When we arrive in late August, house keys are on the dining room table of our rented apartment, courtesy of Francesca, along with all the documents she received at the closing, gathered in a notebook. I stare for a moment in disbelief. They are keys to a house that now officially belongs to us. A house we have seen only twice but have pored over for hours in photos.

We drop our luggage, grab the keys, and dash up the street. While the ancient door must have an ancient key, we have four modern keys to the smaller door of the apartment entrance, with no instruction on how to use them. Four locks are placed in random spots on the door.

"You'd better try." I hand the keys to Jess.

He is far more patient with the inner workings of delicate lock parts. I have been known to break off keys in locks. He tries several combinations with studied patience, intricately maneuvers two keys, and finally the lock clicks open.

As much as I want to see the house, the terrace beckons with a gentle breeze and that expansive view of the valley below, our own panorama of Tuscany. Jess's fig tree is a week or two away from bearing fruit, but the plum tree is ripe now; the ground

below is a carpet of dark purple, more luxurious than any Persian rug, with plums that have already reached perfection and dropped.

Upstairs is filled with furniture—our Italian furniture! The remaining chairs, tables, daybeds, wardrobes, and chest of drawers make it feel like a home. After the first whirlwind jaunt through the house, I take a second, much closer look and discover a hole in the floor of the living area.

A piece of furniture covered it during the viewing back in May, but we weren't exactly examining things in detail. The hole doesn't go all the way through the floor, but the terrazzo is broken, and it looks like water damage from a window left open. I mentally add it to the list for whoever we find who can build kitchen cupboards for us.

∞

In what must have been Gaetana's bedroom, the large bed has a fabric headboard covered in plastic, and bedcovers in a matching pattern still enclose the mattress, made up as if she might return for the evening.

I sit down on the bed and dust whooshes up, dancing in the sunlight from the window. The fabric is faded from the sun, and when I push my finger on it, the threads of the bedcover separate from dry rot. Did Gaetana die in the house, her spirit ascending into eternity from this very room? The walls will not give up all their secrets.

I could stay in the house all day, but Jess has already left, and the desire for sustenance and the company of my husband compels me to leave it for now.

Back at Francesca's apartment, while Jess reads a book and drifts in and out of jet-lag naps, I put the moka pot on for an afternoon coffee. I am eager to dive into the large notebook of closing documents Francesca left for us. It has information on the house; the most interesting document is the property deed that traces the noble family's ownership from Gaetana's father to his daughter and then, with no children of her own, to her nephew by marriage. Gaetana's will is included, naming her nephew as sole heir to her estate.

I have only copies, of course, but they even included a copy of the envelope that held her four-page handwritten will on lined paper. There are important seals, and a large signature trailing the side of each page instead of being limited to one spot at the end of the document as is tradition on most American documents I've seen.

While my Italian is not up to legal documents written in cursive, I can make out through some of the additional pages that Gaetana was born in Torrita di Siena on August 31, 1911.

Gaetana had no children, and I feel an immediate kinship with her. I do have children, of course, but I didn't give birth to them. We are a unique club, this group of women who were designed by God to give birth and yet can't or don't. We have our own heartbreaks for those reasons, and yet we are also spared certain heartbreaks. The depth of joy and sorrow must be heightened when a piece of your own flesh and blood becomes an entirely other person who has an entirely other life. Maybe that's why my mother is always asking me: "Are you going to leave me now?"

Here I go, imagining more than is on the page, which simply says she had no biological heirs. She may have lost a child, either by miscarriage or by having a son or daughter who predeceased her. I am also trying to piece together why it is her nephew "by marriage." Would that be her husband's nephew because she had no nieces or nephews of her own? Or was it her niece's husband? To some it may not matter, but I need to know, because this house chose me, and I want to care for its history.

The pot is gurgling, so I pour a cup and sit back down to continue reading.

The deed tells me the upstairs apartment was renovated in 1952 by Gaetana—only seven years after the trauma of World War II, and she lived there until her death. I surmise that she, as a Mucciarelli heir, was willed or possibly chose the stable for her inheritance and created the living space above it, in what had likely been the hayloft.

I read on to find the date of Gaetana's death: October 23, 2006. This surprises me, since on our first viewing of the house it seemed as if she had only recently died. While the story of Gaetana's life must have many more rich details that I hope to fill in at some point, my reading has brought to light two new pieces of information, and I am not exactly sure what to make of them: The apartment was created in 1952, and it has sat empty for eleven years.

I file the information away because tonight we are going to celebrate. We take a picnic of salami, prosciutto, pecorino cheese, olives, and bread, along with sparkling water and prosecco, up to our new house. We plan to eat on our sunny terrace on this unusually cool August evening.

Jess opens the grand wooden door that leads out to the terrace, and we are met by a chill wind. I will later come to know this as the occasional *tramontana*, the cool wind that comes from the mountains, but this knowledge is not yet in my hands, and the only thing to do is to cross arms and shiver. My hair whips around, stinging me in the face. Eating on the terrace isn't going to work tonight, so we snug our chairs back inside, close enough to enjoy the view but out of the cutting wind. I lay our picnic supper out on the seat of a dusty wooden chair.

Back in May, there were clear blue skies, bright sunshine, and a gentle breeze. A slight shadow of foreboding crosses my mind, but I push it away when Jess pops the bottle of prosecco, and we toast the new house in paper cups.

Jess offers a prayer: "May God be honored, may it be a blessing to others, may we steward it well."

༄

The next morning, I am rested and ready to outline a plan. I grab a pen, a notebook, brew more steaming Lavazza coffee to counter jetlag, and then I settle into my favorite spot on the couch. Today we begin a new work. Not a book this time, but a story just the same: our story in Tuscany.

In keeping with our goals of using the house right away, I plan to return in October with a friend for a short trip so we can paint the walls and furnish

the house with goods beyond the furniture we currently have. Then the apartment will be ready in the spring for us to use ourselves, and share with family and friends, in keeping with our hopes that this house will be an extension of our love for hospitality.

We need two good beds to start, since the dry-rotted mattress in Gaetana's room is not an option, so I write that down as priority number one.

We also need a kitchen. Currently, there are only four tiled walls, since whatever kitchen was here during Gaetana's time has been removed. While this seems strange to us, we've learned that in Italy, the kitchen doesn't normally come with the house, meaning there's no guarantee you will have any cabinets or countertops, and you will most definitely not have any appliances unless you have negotiated them into the purchase.

In fact, when remodeling a kitchen, Italians tend to tile all the way down to the floor behind appliances with the assumption that those appliances will go when the house sells. This way, new owners can change the layout to suit their needs.

I send an email to a local handyman and set up a meeting for the following day. We also have appointments scheduled with two architects to make sure the house has no structural problems and to consider ideas for the possible future renovation of the downstairs stable.

I drain the last of my coffee and rouse Jess from his jet-lagged slumber. Time for action.

∞

La dolce vita, or the sweet life, is ever present in Italy, but the sweet sleep is elusive. Very few times have I experienced a really comfortable bed in Italy, yet they must exist. Beyond comfort, there are the sizes to contend with. Italy calls a twin bed a single. Two twins strapped together to make a king is called a double. There is also something called a *matrimoniale*, which I take to be the king as a whole bed and not two twins pushed together. It seems the size of a *matrimoniale* can vary from what we would consider a queen up to a king size.

We drive to Sinalunga, about twenty minutes away, where we find a mattress store that carries memory-foam mattresses. We meet the father and son who own the business. Once past introductions, we quickly realize their English is as limited as our Italian. This surprises me. Then, as breaking dawn suddenly sheds light on the landscape, I realize that in Italy, English is for tourists, and tourists don't buy mattresses.

Through hand gestures and butchered pronunciations, we select and pay for two mattresses. They must be special ordered but will be delivered in early October, before I will arrive for the final furnishing of the apartment. Perfect timing, or so I think.

That afternoon, Leo walks with me to the center of Montefollonico's piazza so we can open an account at Monte dei Paschi. We didn't look into any other banks even though my husband is in the banking business, deciding that the oldest bank in the world in the middle of our local piazza is good enough for us.

The tiny branch in Montefollonico has somehow fended off the small-town closures since the 2008 crisis, and I am glad it is here. The entrance foyer includes a person-sized tube that resembles something on a 1960s science-fiction show.

We take turns standing in the tube while it closes on one side and then opens on the other, allowing one person in at a time. We then sit down on a bench and wait our turn for the bank clerk to notice us and invite us forward.

This happens when she glances at us and raises an eyebrow. We approach and Leo speaks to her in Italian.

She nods and clicks away on the keyboard as she squints and frowns into the screen behind fashionable glasses. The printer spits out papers, which she gathers and lays before me to sign. I have no idea what I am signing, but I scribble away under Leo's guidance.

She nods again and I take that as a sign we are almost finished, so I ask Leo to ask her about direct billing, something I will need to arrange for all the utilities. I am told I must wait for bills to arrive, except the electric can be done here, mysteriously, without a bill. Clickety-clack on the keyboard, another printout with more signatures, and now my electric bill will automatically be deducted.

This waiting on bills gives me a bit of anxiety since I won't be here to collect them. Who will check the mailbox? I remember to request debit cards, which elicits more tapping on the keyboard.

"Some checks, too, please."

"In Italy, we don't use checks," Leo says.

"No checks? How do I pay bills?"

"All Italians use wire transfer or the bank card. No checks."

Wire transfers are complicated and expensive procedures. How is this going to work?

"You will see," he reassures me.

Before we leave, I am told how to set up my online account, another very important thing for me to know as we manage this new venture from across the sea.

There is now property insurance to buy, and Leo recommends a man who lives in Siena but has roots in Montefollonico. He comes to the house, looks it over, then comes back with the policy, which we sign, again having no idea what the document actually says. The fee is modest, but there is nothing in the house at this point. He suggests that after the remodel we can update the policy.

I let this comment go since I am sure he assumes that, since we are foreigners, we intend to remodel the house. He doesn't understand the house is perfectly fine with us, since our needs are minimal and we like its characteristic charm, but there's no sense in arguing this point.

After Leo leaves, we make an appointment to see Alfonso, which involves asking Francesca to call Alfonso and asking Francesca to be there for the meeting to translate. We are helpless babes.

I wonder if, when I see Alfonso again, I will feel the same uncanny sense of familiarity or if it was simply a one-time imagining under the spell of the Tuscan summer. He arrives early, buzzing up in his shiny green Ape, and yes, he is so very like my uncle Addison.

I initiate the more familial cheek kiss on both sides since it seems right. He isn't put off—in fact, I think he is pleased. Francesca isn't here yet, but Alfonso begins talking. While I can pick up some Italian words, his Tuscan accent is so heavy that I am only catching about one word in fifteen.

I keep saying, "*Sì, sì,*" having no idea what I am saying yes to, yet unable to utter anything else.

Francesca arrives, and I want to hug her with relief. She begins to translate our questions about the house and the baffling myriad of tanks and pipes. When I come back without Jess, I need to know how to make sure we have heat, electricity, and water.

There is a long discussion in Italian between Alfonso and Francesca about pumps for water and pumps for fuel, and then we are informed there is a broken pump.

Alfonso has us follow him to a large diesel tank that sits inside the house on the unfinished ground floor, hidden behind a wall of bricks, with an opening about five feet up, accessed by a ladder. I climb the ladder to peer down in it.

It's the size of a large propane tank that might sit beside a farmhouse in rural Kentucky. I am familiar with something like this outside a house, but inside? This may be commonplace for some people, but it looks downright dangerous to me. How did I miss this when we toured the house back in May?

Alfonso climbs up on a ladder next to the tank and dips a stick into it. He decides there is enough fuel for heat to get us through October when I'm here. I watch his every move, slightly dismayed that dropping a dipstick into a fuel tank will be one of my future chores for the house. After he checks the fuel, he comes down from the ladder and turns to a group of pipes and what looks very much like a car motor. He pulls a lever here, flips a switch there, and the motor fires. He smiles and motions with his hands as if this is no problem.

Jess is not mechanical, technical, or handy. These kinds of hands-on jobs fall to me, which might explain the rising panic I feel as I watch all these foreign machines chug to life.

We move to the water system, which is another mangle of pipes, tanks, and pumps. The plumber is called to examine the broken pump. He says it must be replaced. He cuts off the water and leaves us with a bill for a hundred euros.

Before Alfonso leaves, I ask him his fee for taking care of the place. He shakes his head, gestures with his hands, and looks as if he is smelling something rotten.

Francesca speaks again in Italian, and it seems the smell has gotten worse. He turns his head away.

Francesca turns to us and quotes a per-hour price, a very fair amount, and I agree.

I wonder if my discussion of money and payment was too American for this older Italian gentleman, but how else am I to sort out these things in such a short time?

After Alfonso leaves, Francesca walks through the house with us, looking again at the furniture that we now own.

"These are Tuscan daybeds," she says, pointing. They are the size of a twin bed, with frames made of primitive pieces of wood, roughly cut and nailed together. Sturdy coiled springs are mounded in the middle and covered in fabric. On top of this, striped mattresses serve to cushion the narrow bed, but it is humped in the middle like a camel's back, as if to purposely torture the sleeper. One wrong toss or turn in the night, and a body might be catapulted out an open window.

I imagine these Tuscan daybeds are filled with postwar dust, but Jess is enamored, and I can tell this is on his keep list. At home, it's not a problem to store things until we decide what to do with them later. Here, that is not an option. We have no storage area, and no idea of where to find such a thing. A battle is impending.

CHAPTER
N⁰ 12

Francesca leaves, and now it's time to meet with Luca, the handyman. I have communicated with Luca on email, and he always responds in English, so I feel confident in releasing Francesca and handling this meeting alone.

Jess has had enough and retreats to our rented apartment to read.

Luca arrives with his phone in his hand, the Google Translate app pulled up, ready to go. He doesn't speak English after all.

"We need some cabinets here," I say, awkwardly enunciating my words. I tend to lop off the end of my words like a sandwich maker might cut off and toss the heel of the bread. The end isn't necessary, or so says my central Kentucky speech pattern.

He frowns when he reads the translation, so I resort to sign language. My twelve weeks of Italian is not enough to explain the floor damage. He follows me into another room where I point to the hole in the floor.

"*Acqua?*"

"*Sì.*" He scratches his chin and grimaces.

Before we can make it back to the kitchen where I intend to draw out the proposed cabinets, he bends down and looks at the electrical outlets. I bend down and look at them too and realize for the first time that they look nothing like the outlets in Francesca's apartment. We stand up at the same time and barely miss hitting our heads together. He frowns and shakes his head.

"*Molti problemi,*" he says and clicks his tongue. Many problems. "*Troppo lavoro.*" I don't understand, so he punches something into his phone and then reads aloud to me in perfectly unaccented English: "Too much for me."

I am trying to understand what the implication of this might be when he mumbles something in Italian and makes a quick exit. I want to ask him who we should talk to about the work, but I don't have the words. I walk in a dazed stupor down to the street to our rented apartment and up the steps where I find Jess reading. He looks up from his book, smiling at me, then his face shifts.

"Are you all right? Ang?"

I pause, take a deep breath, then decide to lay it all out. "The apartment needs total electrical work. It's not up to code. The kitchen is the only thing that's been rewired, but we still need a design for it. There's the hole in the floor and the water issue that caused it. Then there's that fuel tank sitting like a bomb below the living quarters." I don't even mention the water pump that needs replacing. That seems like a small thing.

He crosses his arms and leans back.

"I'm glad we set up meetings with the two architects. We need help now, not for some future project."

He takes a deep breath and raises his eyebrows. I don't say the dreaded "R" word but I know we both realize we are careening down renovation road.

"In the meantime, I'd love to get outside and do something in the sunshine. We could free those terrace stones from the weeds."

He brightens at the idea of physical work. "Let's get some tools!"

We hop in the car with a mission but realize we don't know where to buy garden tools. At home, I would drive into town to Boone's Hardware, but we don't even know how to say *hardware* in Italian.

"I think I remember seeing something that looked like a hardware store in the next village," I say, as we head down the mountain. We learn the word, *ferramenta*, and find one on the main road, buy picks and trowels, drive back up the mountain, and attack the weeds with gusto. We pick away at the grass and dirt that have nearly covered the ancient stones. Our new Italian neighbors call greetings over the fence. We call back and resume work, the sun warm on our backs, for now pushing away the disappointment.

Jess has two personalities when it comes to a renovation. There is the banker, who is always interested in the least amount of expense. Then there is the artist, who is more concerned with aesthetics and the beauty of a plan. In his perfect world, he would have the artistic achievements at a banker's price. This rarely happens in reality, and the usual outcome in our early days of doing remodels together was going with the banker price on the front end, only to end up redoing parts of the project later. This ends up costing more money, which of course defeats the purpose.

My weakness when embarking on renovations is the endless world of "what if." What if we opened up a door here or put a window there? Should we paint this and rebuild that? But there's usually a hefty price tag attached to that way of thinking. In the past, we've learned that when the artistic side of Jess shows up, we are arm-in-arm singing and clinking glasses: *cin-cin!* When the banker shows up, a cold wind blows between us, and we are crossed arms and frowns.

As we await our first architect, Jess is all banker, and rightly so. We are wrapping our brains around the idea that there are *molti problemi* related to this house and exactly what this means for our plan of creating a guesthouse to use soon and share with our friends and family.

Architect Adriano arrives in short sleeves and khaki shorts and swings a clipboard at his side. It's smack in the middle of the Italian holiday, the two weeks between *Ferragosto* and the end of August, and it's a pleasant surprise that he can even meet with us. Yet Adriano is here, bright-eyed and eager to see the building.

Jess sets up our goals with his "fast and cheap" speech. We want to do the least amount of work possible to make the upstairs as livable as quickly as we can. Then we would like a plan to redo the downstairs area in the future. The idea of a phase one and phase two, as we have come to terms with a renovation.

We start with the second-floor apartment. He shakes his head and mumbles the word *tutto* as he walks around, jotting notes on the clipboard.

"What about this?" Jess points to the hole in the floor.

Adriano shrugs. "If you want to keep this flooring, then it can be repaired."

"What about the diesel tank on the first floor?" I say. Surely this must be an essential thing to remove, phase one. Adriano looks around, confused. "Where?"

"On the first floor," I enunciate as clearly as I can. I am beginning to detest my Southern accent.

"This floor?"

"No, the first floor. Downstairs."

"Ahh, *piano terra*, the ground floor."

"What is this floor called?" I point to the second floor.

"*Primo piano*, the first floor." He looks at me as if it were a trick question, and we go downstairs to the *piano terra*. He doesn't seem surprised to see a diesel tank inside a structure. He grunts and makes more notes. "It is better not be here."

Outside on the terrace, the sun is shining, but the dark clouds of reality gather.

"What do you think?" Jess crosses his arms and plants his feet as if bracing himself. "How much will it cost?" The American is coming out now. Give me the bottom line, no dancing around.

Adriano saves us from the shock. "Let me do some figuring. Come to my office tomorrow and we can talk more. But I think two phases is not a good idea. It's better to do all at once."

Dinner that night is somber. We've done enough renovations to know that tackling the whole thing at once will save time, money, and later aggravation. Our dream of moving in right away, of enjoying the house next year, has dried up like a Vin Santo grape.

∽

There are no lights on in Adriano's office, unlike the fluorescent glare that is ever-present in most American offices, but the natural light from the window is enough. We sit in a room that serves as conference room and drafting room. Adriano's achievements and accolades are framed and hung on the wall.

Jess jumps right in with the first place we start with any renovation. "How much of the roof needs repairing?"

"*Tutto*," says Adriano. The whole thing.

Jess goes pale and covers his head with his hands.

"No problem," Adriano says quickly. "All in one day—not expensive."

"What about that terrazzo floor?" I ask, since I don't like the terrazzo, which reminds me of a 1950s public building. When we were thinking of moving in, a few well-placed rugs would soften the look. But if we're doing a complete restoration to the upstairs, this is the perfect opportunity to repair the hole by replacing the floor.

A long and confusing discussion ensues while he breaks into a mix of Italian and English and says "outside" several times. I can't understand why he is talking about the outside.

Finally, when we are both about to pull out our hair, he asks me, "What this mean to you, *terrazzo*?" I point to the polished pebble-and-cement floor and the light goes on. "Ahh, okay. In *Italiano*, *terrazzo* means terrace." We both laugh at the misunderstanding. In the end, he makes a case for repairing it rather than replacing it. Jess is still pale, so I concede.

I share my idea of moving the kitchen to the back of the upstairs apartment so the view can be enjoyed from there. Then I raise an issue that I've been tipped off to by a couple of expat Americans who stopped by one day when I was at the house. They told me, "Don't let the architect move your sink away from the window. Italians never put sinks in front of windows." It never crossed my mind, but now that I think about it, the apartment that we rent does not have the sink in front of a window. I ask Adriano about this.

"The sink is problem," he says. "You must open the window and is problem for you if the sink is there. All my Italy customers want sink in front of window like Americans but is problem. Can't reach out far enough to open window in Italy. Not push up window like in America." I concede, again. But while we're on American preferences, I raise the issue of a clothes dryer.

"Is problem. In Italy, we have limited energy, not like America with much

116

energy for many things. Here, it is conserved and, when you use it, is very expensive. For dryer, too much. Italians hang clothes outside. Dries very fast."

I can tell I'm going to lose a lot of battles if we go forward with this, but at the end of the day, I would be happy to have a shed in Italy, so I'm willing to compromise. Adriano will work on some figures and get back to us in a week.

In the meantime, I set about sorting through the furniture and what we want to keep and what we can give away. Jess has expressed admiration for every item we acquired from the house purchase, including the faded and broken-down director's chair that he is convinced can be repaired and used on the terrace.

I have a pile of items I am quite sure we will never use, and I appeal to his generous nature. "Someone else could really use these things."

Jess reluctantly agrees, but one point of contention is the Tuscan daybeds, or the catapults, as I call them. I can appreciate their value, historically, as an improvement over sleeping on the floor or among the animals. But as interesting as these artifacts are, I cannot see any scenario where they would be useful to us. There are six of them.

We compromise by selecting the two best to keep for now and gifting the others. The pile to give away grows larger, but the director's chair stays with us.

I ask Francesca and Alfonso to invite the villagers to take from the pile. Our request is met with a shrug and disinterest, but miraculously, the small mountain is diminished considerably in only a few days.

Three Tuscan daybeds and an assortment of other items from the pile remain. Francesca suggests an organization in Siena that operates much like our Salvation Army. They have to be called first with a list of the items to be picked up, and then we are assigned a pickup day. There seems to be a procedure for everything here, from garbage collection and recycling to giving items away, which makes me think twice about consumption. The very point, I assume.

Lorenzo, the other architect we contacted, arrives with an assistant. He's recently back from his August vacation, tan, with a crisp white shirt and styled grayish-white hair. He's from Florence but has some family connections to the area.

He stops us inside the door. "I must tell you, I know this house." This is not unusual, we are finding out. Many people know the house because of Gaetana, who lived here over fifty years. The next part is surprising.

"In fact, I made an offer on it that was higher than your offer, but I had some contingencies. I don't know why my offer was not accepted." He shrugs as if it doesn't matter. "I've even drawn up plans if you care to see them, or I can tell you what I envisioned."

Well, this changes everything. Here is a man with a detailed, premeditated plan! Adriano is fading from my memory.

"Please show us," I say, and he unfolds a roughly drawn sketch of the plans. We start walking and envisioning what Lorenzo has designed. When we reach the second floor—or as the Italians say, the first floor—I ask Lorenzo about the terrazzo.

"It should be replaced." Finally, a voice of reason. Lorenzo confirms the renovations must all be done at once. He says it's impossible to live on the second floor while work is going on downstairs. What's more, he says it will be a two-year job.

Two years. My heart sinks. Jess is pushing for a number, but like the other architect, Lorenzo promises to do some figuring. He and his assistant leave, and we shut the door behind them.

❦

Jess has the dejected look of someone who is intent on having a peanut butter sandwich and is now being told only prime rib is available. He only wants the peanut butter.

I thought I wanted peanut butter too. But now I am smelling the prime rib. "Did you hear what he said about a pergola outside?"

"I only heard two years."

"Remember what we learned on all our efforts to revitalize Stanford: Do it right the first time. If we have to go back and redo things later, that's additional time the house can't be used and more expense. What are the chances we would interview an architect who likes the house so much he made an offer on it and drew up plans?"

"Two years," Jess reminds me.

The numbers arrive from both architects, and Lorenzo is higher, as we anticipated.

Adriano's personality is an easy fit for us, yet I am concerned he will sacrifice quality for the sake of being fast and cheap. Jess anticipates battles ahead with Lorenzo.

"He may be too invested in the house," Jess says when I wave the pre-drawn plans as a sign he might be the one. What I see as a positive, Jess sees as negative. We are at an impasse and have only two weeks left to decide the future of the house. The only thing to do is pray for guidance, something we should have done in the beginning.

CHAPTER

N͟o 13

The village is bustling with people who have come from Rome, Milan, and even America back to the family village for the summer holidays, and we are swept up in the active social life of Montefollonico, a welcome distraction from the conundrum of the house.

Francesca and Benedetta are delighted we have bought the house and will be neighbors. Other neighbors that we don't know as well now greet us with smiles as we pass on the street. Francesca says we are now *montanini*, or inhabitants of Montefollonico, a sign of acceptance.

Are they really happy to have Americans edging into their beautiful Italian town? Are we invading the pristine village to change it for the worse? I surely hope not. It would be the worst kind of irony to want to participate in something so lovely and, by the very act of participation, change it. I hope we can contribute with humility and grace.

When talk of the house comes up, we hear an expression over and over from friends and acquaintances on the street: *piano, piano.*

"Francesca, what does *piano, piano* mean?" I ask her one day in her art studio. I could look it up, but I find a native speaker can provide much more nuance.

"Ah, it means slowly, slowly, or bit by bit."

The other phrase we hear is *molto lavoro*, or much work. The Italians knew all along this was going to be a big job.

One lazy, hot afternoon, we pass by the bar and see Alfonso sitting with a group of men around a plastic card table under the shade of the linden trees. He looks up and acknowledges us, and Jess takes this as an invitation to watch the card game. They are playing *tresettes*, one of the most common card games in Italy, and Jess wants to learn.

I order a coffee and seat myself away from the men, allowing them to have their male bonding time. What does Alfonso think of us, these Americans who might bring strange ideas to disrupt the house he has known for so many years? We have learned that his wife helped Gaetana inside the house, so they are both more than caretakers—they are investors in the house and in the village. Whatever we end up doing with the house, I want to make sure it remains a Tuscan house and not an Americanized home, even if that means giving up a window over the sink and a clothes dryer. Well, at least the window over the sink.

❧

Our Italian neighbors, Fausto and Viviana, speak machine-gun Italian, are fit and trim at eightysomething, and glow vitamin D. Their backyard connects to ours and is separated by a wire fence. One of their sons, Vito, is a former world-class track and field star. Vito technically is our true next-door neighbor, but he doesn't have a yard, so Fausto and Viviana are the ones we see the most when we are outside examining the house.

One afternoon, we run into them on the street, and they offer to show us their houses, which we find are actually connected on the inside. While our house was the stable for the Mucciarelli family, Vito's apartment was the granary, or the *granaio*, and has a hall that connects through a doorway to his parents' house. Fausto and Viviana live in Rome most of the time but spend the summers in Montefollonico.

We learn that Fausto is a retired firefighter. Vito shows us a picture on his phone of Fausto doing a handstand on the beach, only the year before. I don't know many people over forty who can do a handstand. It is an impressive sight.

Village life seems to be good for longevity; many *montanini* are over ninety and even a few over a hundred. Italian village life is assisted living without the institution. Instead of bingo, the most popular activity is people-watching at the village gate or in the piazza, along with playing cards at the bar. Short walks to the market for food and news, or longer walks to the cemetery outside the village, provide physical activity. There are also slow walks around the playground to smile at the children, occasional bocce games in the park, and watching soccer games on the TV at the bar. On Sundays at eleven o'clock in the morning and every day at five o'clock in the afternoon there is Mass.

Multigenerational interaction is available for all, with all the stimulation that provides. We often see Fausto and Viviana taking advantage of all these activities, but their favorite seems to be morning coffee at the bar with their friends, where the chatter is animated.

On the other side of our house is the former restaurant where we first saw the view off to Cortona. We have heard that a British couple has bought the property and are making it into their home.

I have imagined them as an older, reserved couple in tweeds and jodhpurs. When they stop in at our new house one day to say hello, I am surprised to find they are close to us in age, friendly and down to earth.

Julia and Trevor both worked as civil servants, are excellent conversationalists, and are both warm and engaging. Julia has a melodious voice, and I could listen to her speak all day. Because we are both beginning similar works, we have much to discuss, so we make plans for dinner a few days later.

Our social calendar is filling up, a stark contrast to our life back in Kentucky. At home, we both are busy during the day with work, people, and responsibilities. When we finally make it home at the end of the day, we often prefer staying on the farm, enjoying a long walk in the summer or a fireside puzzle in the winter. Most of our friends live miles away.

We are so much closer to people here, with our roofs literally connected. It is only natural to gather together either at the bar for a midmorning coffee or around six or six thirty for *la passeggiata*, the time before dinner when everyone goes for a social walk or a chat.

Montefollonico's bar is where friends gather to discuss the events of the day, where new babies are admired, dogs are petted, cards are played, and newspapers are read. It's where the sports channel plays the big soccer games; if the game is really big and the weather is good, the television is passed through the window and propped on a table outside for a larger crowd.

Now that we have bought property here, I am amazed how many of the locals want to usher me inside to see their homes. This is a delightful surprise, walking on the street one minute and the next minute sipping an espresso or prosecco in someone's apartment or house—a person who speaks no English but is not the least bit deterred by my bumbling Italian.

This never happened to me as a tourist. Somehow the return visits, the gradual familiarity, and the recent stamp of love for the village by buying a house gives me membership into a club, and finally, a seat at the table I longed for when we first came here a few years ago.

❧

There are new discoveries every day. For one, we realize now that Giuseppina prepares lunch items on certain days of the week at the market, including lasagna, stewed white beans, and *ribollita*, a hearty Tuscan stew. Pizza is only eaten for dinner here, so if you want a pizza from the market, the order must be placed at lunch and then picked up at seven thirty, but only on Wednesdays and Saturdays.

The pizzas are prepared ahead but not put in the oven until a customer comes in the market. Whichever daughter is at the cash register spots an arrival and yells their name to Giuseppina in the deli, who calls it back to the other daughter in the mysterious hidden room where food is stored—and where, apparently, there is a pizza oven. Minutes later, the customer is handed a hot pizza in a steaming box. This is not greasy, gooey American pizza but more of a flat crust with a coating of tomato sauce, a light smattering of cheese, and a scattering of either vegetables or cured meat.

It's Thursday, not pizza day, when Isabella waves me to the meat counter.

"We have *porchetta*," she says with a smile. "Would you like?" She knows we are keen to try anything local.

"*Sì*." My eyes are wide, as I watch her slice pieces off a roll of meat, with fat and skin, and what looks like spices rolled into the middle of it. There is no bone, but it's as large and round as a football and about a foot long. This is a majestic hunk of meat.

She wraps the slices and hands the package to me over the top of the deli counter. "Take with a glass of red wine." She makes a sign with her hands to indicate that's all. "*Semplice*." Simple.

I carry the treasure home to Jess, and we do exactly as Isabella recommends, as if it were a doctor's prescription. It is delicious, moist and rich with spices against the rustic dark cherry flavor of the Vino Nobile wine from nearby Montepulciano. I lean back in the shade of the porch, deeply satisfied with the food, the warm embrace of the community, and the idea of possessing a tiny part of this ancient land.

My dreamy state is interrupted with this last thought. What are we going to do about the house? My eyes fly open, and I sit bolt upright. While we have been flitting about from *aperitivo* invitations to coffee meets and card games, precious days are slipping by, and soon we will be on a plane home.

I look over at Jess, who is resting peacefully on the outdoor settee, enjoying his own shut-eyed version of the afternoon *riposino*. We've not yet had a conversation about what happens if we can't move forward with a reasonable answer to this dilemma.

Do we cut our losses and let go of the dream?

CHAPTER No 14

We meet Trevor and Julia at a pizzeria a couple of miles from the village and are seated on the terrace under a star-filled August night sky. They are easy company, and we find so much to talk about.

"Be prepared when selecting paint colors in Montefollonico. Everything is yellow," Julia says. "When they ask for your color preference, understand the question is not the color, because that will of course be yellow—they are asking for the shade of yellow."

"I wish I were simply talking about shades of yellow," I say.

We have quickly gone from polite talk to spilling out the angst of our project and our architect dilemma over dinner to our new fast friends and future neighbors. As the *antipasti* plates are removed, Trevor asks us an important question.

"What is your end goal? Do you envision it more for a residence or a holiday house?"

"We like the idea of spending more time here, but we also see it as a guesthouse for our friends and family," Jess says.

Then a question from Julia that really makes us think: "Do you really need an architect? If you have a good idea of what you want to do, maybe it's not necessary."

"Who would manage the renovation?" This is a key question for me since I certainly can't do it from America, nor do I know the language or the culture.

"A good *geometra* can do it," Julia says.

"I've never heard of a *geometra*," I confess.

"It's similar to an architect, but with less of a focus on creative design and more hands-on responsibilities. A *geometra* does the drawings, manages all the permits, and makes sure everything is up to code," Trevor explains.

"One of the architects mentioned something about permits taking six months or more."

"We've heard there are forty-two parts to the approval process for any outside changes to historic houses inside a medieval village," Julia says.

Forty-two approvals. One document with forty-two checkpoints? Forty-two stamps needed, or signatures, or even just initials? Will it be mailed, or hand carried? Maybe someone will spill coffee on it or drop some crumbs from a *bombolone*. Maybe it will land on the desk of someone who is on vacation, or perhaps has an illness and is out for a couple of weeks. I imagine this frayed, crumbled, and spotted document when it finally reaches the end of the gauntlet, and I feel sorry for it.

We are nearing the end of dinner when we ask Julia and Trevor how long they have been married. They say they have a significant anniversary coming up the following summer.

"We do too," I say. "It will be our twentieth."

"Really? Ours too!" Julia says.

"What month?"

"July. And yours?"

"July! What day?"

"The eighteenth," I say.

"Ours too!"

We compare the time we were married, and considering the time change between the United Kingdom and Kentucky, we find out we married within one hour of each other. Here we are, two couples from different continents married on the same day living next door to each other in a Tuscan village. It seems unbelievable and yet so perfectly appointed.

⌾

The next day, we turn our attention back to our dilemma and Julia's very interesting comment. We always use an architect, but that's often because we are making outside changes with our renovation projects. Maybe in this situation, it is not necessary after all.

I hope our new pastor friend, Giacomo, might shed some light on our situation. He is bringing his father, Rocco, to meet us. Rocco is a lay pastor and has some building experience.

We wait for Rocco and Giacomo at the bar. When they arrive, I'm struck by how little alike they appear. Giacomo is taller while Rocco is more compact. Rocco has a firm handshake and steady, sharp eyes. Giacomo has gentle eyes and a ready smile. I sense how very complementary they are to each other.

Over coffee under the linden trees, we find out Rocco has renovated several of his own properties. The rental income allows him to serve the church without a salary as a lay pastor. Jess, who was already eager to meet Rocco, immediately connects with a fellow entrepreneur.

After coffee, we take him through the house, where I see hints of an exacting personality and high standards. He shakes his head at some things that must be fixed, and for things that are really bad, he shakes his finger.

With Giacomo interpreting, he hits on every important thing Lorenzo has said must be done. We look at the infamous hole in the upstairs floor. This, for me, is the real test.

"What about this?" I ask innocently, pointing to the crumbling terrazzo.

"*No, no. Deve essere tutto sostituito.*" It all must be replaced, he says. No hesitation. I give Jess a triumphant look, and he reluctantly nods in agreement.

Rocco studies the walls, knocks on the plaster, squats to peer in the wine vats, and dismisses some things with a wave of his hand. He admires the terra-cotta ceilings, muses on the stone behind the plaster, and scowls at the mass of concrete on the terrace. When he looks at the view, he crosses his arms and relaxes into a broad smile.

"How long should this project take, to do the whole thing?" Jess asks, and we both brace for the answer.

Rocco shrugs. "*Un anno*," he says. A year. This might have been shocking to us a couple of weeks ago, but we've already adjusted to the idea of two years. With the work that needs to be done and wait time for the coffee-stained forty-two approvals, one year sounds miraculous.

"How much should it cost?" Rocco ponders the question and then flashes several fingers. Despite his minimal Italian, Jess immediately gets it. His gift for numbers apparently transcends languages. Jess makes a great show of shock. Rocco is not fazed by Jess's dramatics, which endears him to me even more. The number is lower than what we heard from Adriano and far lower than Lorenzo's quote, but he is giving us an idea without architect fees tacked on.

I ask about the forty-two permits. "Six to eight months for outside work," Giacomo translates. "It's possible to do work inside before then. Those permits are faster and only a few are required."

I wonder how many are "a few."

"Rocco, can we do this without an architect?"

"*Sì*," Rocco says. He speaks more in Italian, and Giacomo translates. "You need a project manager and a good *geometra*."

"What would a good project manager charge?" Jess asks.

"*Tre o quattro per cento*," Rocco says with a shrug. Three to four percent. Jess extends his hand. "Four percent to manage the project."

Giacomo translates as Jess locks eyes with Rocco. There is a moment of surprise, hesitation, and then Rocco grasps Jess's hand in agreement.

I walk with Giacomo to their car after lunch.

"Does your dad really want to do this?"

"This will be good for my father," Giacomo says. I realize he doesn't answer my question.

After a day goes by, I begin to relax. Rocco strikes me as the kind of man who would let us know quickly if he had second thoughts.

⌐∞⌐

As our time in Tuscany on this pivotal trip draws to a close, we spend the last week in Italy with the Harpers, friends who have come to visit Montefollonico at our invitation. Jess and I have both known Todd a long time, but our meetings with Collynn have been brief. We enjoy getting to know her better, and we tell endless stories about Davis, their oldest son, who recently finished a stint as one of Jess's interns. The Harpers live in Florida, but Davis decided he likes our part of the country and is staying on in the area even though his internship is completed.

Before we leave, Alfonso brings us a gift of home made Vin Santo from 1996, a piece of paper taped on the bottle with the year. I hug him and feel the warmth of this strange phenomenon I have experienced less than a handful of times in my life. It is a gift from God that says, "Here's this new person in your life, but you already know him."

If our house was complete, I would leave the bottle here. But soon it will be a construction site and no place for the valuable gift. I pack it carefully in my suitcase for the trip home.

Was it only three weeks ago when we arrived thinking we could paint and nail together some shelves in the kitchen? We are headed into a yearlong restoration project, the exact enterprise we did not want to undertake. Yet there is mysterious peace in the midst of it, as if we are on a track laid out for us long ago. There have been too many helps along the way, too many open doors, even when the journey took strange turns.

I have a strong sense there will be more to come.

CHAPTER
N<u>o</u> 15

I thought you were trying to cut things out of your life," my friend says over the phone, when I tell her about the renovation project. This is not just any friend but someone who has known me for years, has listened to me moan repeatedly about the length of my to-do list, and can speak truth in my life. We are also very different people. If she has two appointments in a day, she believes it is a full day. For me, two appointments are simply what a full day is scheduled around.

"Don't you have a book launch this fall?"

"Yeah, but that's in November. The big work on the house won't get going until the spring, and I'll be finished with book commitments by then." The silence on the other end of the line tells me she is not convinced.

It is strange to reconcile seeking rest with taking on a large-scale renovation project an ocean away, in another language, another currency, and another measurement system, so I understand her silence.

A hard workout can be restful to a doctor who needs to be outside the medical office, and the same is true for me. I don't need more sleep or even physical rest; I need more time for the things that give my mind and spirit life instead of sapping them. The renovation itself may be stressful, but I am motivated to do it because when it is over we will have our own haven in a restful and inspiring corner of the world.

Jess has even warmed to the idea. It's not a peanut butter sandwich, but it's not prime rib either. While the financial commitment is significant, we have worked hard to stay out of debt and build our savings. Jess feels confident in Rocco's ability to watch the bottom line, and even Howard is fully on board.

As to the pruning, well, that does remain elusive for the time being. A yes in one area does mean a no in others. For one, I have realized I can't start another book during this process since my creative writing time will be channeled into creation of another sort.

There is still no solution for pruning out the many day-to-day business responsibilities, despite our multiple discussions. Still, the project renews my hope and forces even more the need for us to find a solution. At least, that is what I tell myself.

Maybe I am lying to myself. Maybe I am afraid to stop being busy.

"It should be fine," I assure my friend. "As long as nothing goes off the rails."

A couple of weeks later, the phone wakes us at six in the morning. Jess answers, and when I realize it is a legitimate phone call, I get up as well. No one makes a social call that early, and I can tell it's serious from his end of the conversation.

"That was Todd. Davis has been in a car accident, and he's in critical condition. I need to go to the hospital and see him."

"Oh no!" I put my hand on my head and try to process what he is saying in the fog of waking up.

Jess looks back at me, and I can tell he is doing the same.

"You need to go." I toss shoes toward him as he springs into action. He dresses quickly and is out the door. Unsure if I should follow him to the hospital or wait for him to call me after he gets there, I decide to dress and am just making my way downstairs when Jess calls me with shattering news.

"Davis died."

∞

Later that afternoon, we pick Todd and Collynn up at the Louisville airport, two parents who have received the worst news anyone can receive, two parents in shock. We go with them to the crash site, sit with them while they talk with the coroner, and receive friends who descend on our house from all points north and south to comfort a much-loved family.

It is a sacred time, and the air is thick with the Holy Spirit's comforting presence. We feed and console, talk and pray, tell stories, laugh, and cry. House renovation plans are trivial in light of this sudden and early departure of a promising young man. Our time in Italy with the Harpers seems like a dreamy mirage. How thankful and amazed I am that God designed the timing so Collynn would be completely comfortable around us after spending time together in Italy only the month prior. I was able to keep her in tea and lip balm, two tiny comforts I learned she appreciated from our time in Italy.

The autumn passes in this swirl of sadness and memorial. Just as the leaves spiral from the trees, we shed once again any idea that we might know what the future holds.

∞

As always with grief, the rest of life moves on, and autumn turns to winter. Decisions to make, work to complete, designs to approve.

The *geometra* is ready to shepherd the famous forty-two permits through the gauntlet of approvals. First, historical research must be conducted in order to build a case for any changes we request. Italy is very strict about historic structures, especially ones located inside medieval walls. Ultimately, the governing body in Siena will make the final decisions on what can be done.

During this process, a pleasant surprise comes when the *geometra* discovers a drawing from the 1200s with evidence of a structure on our site. We are shown a tiny photograph of a pencil sketch on yellow paper, fascinating and cryptic, a connection from the past to the present.

When winter finally releases its icy grip, we arrive in Montefollonico to a cold, slicing March wind that cuts up and down the village street despite the deception of bright sunshine. We settle into Francesca's apartment and then peek inside the house, hoping to see activity but finding only a quiet pile of rubble.

An official document is posted on the front of the house announcing the intent of reconstruction. It lists my full name, Angela Betty Correll, along with Jess's full name, the name of the *geometra*, the name of the construction company, the local officials who approved the project, and the amount of money we have agreed to pay the construction company for the work. So much for privacy.

For most of my life, I have worked to bury my middle name, my own mother's name, which felt to me like a holdover from the 1950s, or maybe the 1930s when my grandmother gifted it to my mother. Soon I will find that Italy displays it on every single legal document and doesn't consider my signature legal without it.

We meet with Giacomo, who guides us, in English, step-by-step in the process, for the next decision Rocco needs from us.

"Next, we must move the furniture out while the work is going," he says.

Where? This feels like an impossible task in Italy, where storage space is at a premium. I turn to Francesca, who always seems to have a solution.

Francesca knows a man who might have suitable space in the village. As with all Italian transactions, there must be a face-to-face meeting with this man first. At home, it could be handled by email or a telephone conversation without ever meeting in person. Not here. We'll be drinking prosecco together before it's over. A meeting, a conversation, then a garage door opens and an empty cantina is revealed, the perfect size for furniture storage.

The demolition begins, and helpers arrive to chisel-tap in a jazzlike rhythm as the ancient stone walls are freed from the crumbling *intonaco*, or plaster. The house looks like a shaken snow globe, dust swirling in place of snow.

Within a couple of days, an ancient arch is uncovered in the entrance room when the *intonaco* is all chipped away. The local historian stops by and estimates the large arch is from the fifteenth century. It is a work of art, now exposed for all to admire. Many neighbors stop by and do just that.

What was a nondescript, plastered, hard-angled entrance into the wine vat room is now revealed as a glorious high-arched doorway. The massive concrete wine vats are gone, and the arched ceilings are now exposed. We nearly fall backward trying to view it all while stumbling over debris on the floor. Jess coughs and I sneeze.

Eventually, the dust will settle and the rubble will be carted away, leaving a clean structure, ready for a new work to begin. One afternoon, I stand in the house, watching the work, and am jarred with the realization of how important this cleaning out is to the entire renovation. It simply must be done. We can't slather new mortar over the old or else the whole thing will crumble. Jesus said the same thing when he talked of pouring new wine into old wineskins.

Am I trying to skip over removing the old plaster when I set new behavioral goals as a way to create this next season of my life? I have this grand idea of pruning, but it has yet to result in the first snip. How can I begin building anew if the old is not torn off first? No wonder I've made no progress at all with the lofty goals I had leading up to my fiftieth birthday.

I touch each brick of the exposed arch and think about my natural desire to stack goal upon goal in the same way these bricks are stacked. Another bar to set, another thing to strive for, another way to be found wanting. If I work hard now, I can rest later, I tell myself—yet later never comes. Round and round it goes, and the performance cycle never ends.

The house inspires me to begin tearing off the behavior patterns to expose the framework underneath: what drives me to stay so busy all the time, to leave no margin for the unexpected things that will happen in life, like sudden tragedies or even simply giving my time to a friend or family member who needs it.

I need to go back to the foundation, to how, where, and when the patterns formed before the pruning can even be done. Otherwise, how will I even know what to prune? In the end, maybe this internal work will reveal something glorious underneath, like the newly exposed arch.

CHAPTER
№ 16

Until recently, I would have said the first loss I experienced was my grandfather passing away when I was nineteen years old. Somehow, I had blocked out the depth of feeling around my uncle Addison's life and death and its impact on me, until I met Alfonso. I knew it intellectually—it wasn't like I forgot that he lived and died—but somehow I disconnected myself emotionally from it. Now that I have given myself permission to remember Uncle Addison through Alfonso, memories come to me in waves from a place in my mind that has spent decades sealed away.

When I was six years old, we took a trip to Virginia Beach, my first time to see the ocean from our landlocked Kentucky. As soon as we stepped onto the beach and the ocean came into view, the expanse of the sea and the mesmerizing lure of the waves drew me to the water, as if cued by the siren. I took off running straight for it, the splash of my feet in the waves drowning out the screams of my mother. I had no intention of stopping. I wanted to be in the water, like a fish going home. I was ankle-deep and then knee-deep before Uncle Addison scooped me up, both of us laughing.

More memories surface from the two trips to Florida, where

I watched my parents and Uncle Addison and Aunt Norma play endless Rook games between time spent in the pool, on the beach, and at seafood feasts. Uncle Addison and I celebrated our back-to-back March birthdays in Florida with cake and souvenir gifts.

I now remember spending every Saturday at his real estate office, where I read comic books and ate honey buns while the adults conducted business. I recall winter evenings when we were glued to the news channel to catch glimpses of Uncle Addison auctioning tobacco at the warehouse in Lexington during the evening tobacco sales report.

Now that I am willing to crack the door to my locked-away memories, even more rise like haunting ghosts from an old family cemetery.

∽

Months after my father turned fifty, and just a couple of weeks after my eighth birthday was celebrated in Florida, a swath of deadly tornadoes swept across thirteen states. I huddled with my parents in our tiny root cellar, listening to news from the radio, while people were killed and destruction reigned only a few short miles away. The next morning, the wind had calmed outside, but something unsettling was brewing inside our house.

There was an undercurrent of tension that swirled just below the surface and periodically erupted with sharp words that flew like darts between my parents, sometimes hitting their mark and sometimes landing on me.

We were a blended family with adult children and now grandchildren who were my age. My parents worked long hours, and with little free time outside of church and work, my mother studied for her real estate exam so she could be a saleswoman.

Praise and attention came my way when I helped around the house, so I learned to do the laundry, to make my own lunch in the summer, to help with supper, to wash the dishes, and to clean the house. Work provided distracted relief from the growing anxiety inside the house, and it made me feel like I was fixing a nebulous and unnamed problem. Reading books from the local bookmobile, the school library, and our church library provided endless escapes into other worlds. Playing with kids in the neighborhood on long summer days filled a longing for siblings my age.

I can now see that my parents were tired, physically and emotionally, and when strange pains and fears seemed to always strike me at bedtime, they were often dismissed with exhausted frustration. I couldn't express what I was feeling and fearing, so I learned to stuff my emotions, to create my own fortress, and to cultivate a calm on the outside no matter what anxieties rattled around inside like skeletal ghosts.

The simmering tensions erupted in June of the following year as the arguments came with more frequency and higher volume, along with my mother's one glorious display of athleticism when she spun a greasy plate across the kitchen like a frisbee, aiming for my father's head. I was too young to understand the adult conflict, but I knew something had happened between my parents that threatened our family as much as that deadly tornado only a year before. One month later, on a hot and humid Tuesday morning, my uncle Addison dropped dead in the threshold of his real estate office from a massive heart attack.

The sudden and shocking news rippled through the community. Friends and neighbors gathered at their home, where my aunt Norma sat on a couch and received condolences through wailing tears. I would never hear her cackling laugh again. The sadness consumed her, and she eventually drifted out of our lives.

There would be no more trips to Florida, no more Saturdays at his office, and no more birthday celebrations together. It was the first real loss in my life, the one that taught me someone you love could be taken from you suddenly and without warning.

With each piece of old plaster I tear off the walls of my heart, I begin to let these painful memories rise up from the hidden place one last time. The words my parents lashed out in the midst of their own pain come to me, and I write them down. Not so I can remember them, but so I can look at them with an adult's heart full of compassion. So I can give them to God in forgiveness. These words don't belong to my parents. They came from a source of pain only God can understand. Then I verbalize the greatest act of love: I forgive. Flames lick and the words disappear. The ashes drift away on the wind, taking my childhood storm with it.

After my uncle Addison died, my parents made peace with each other, as if his death pushed them together. It was a hard and a bumpy road for a long while after that, but they finally found a rhythm. My parents continued to work together into their eighties. They became inseparable until death did them part, and for that I am most grateful.

❧

I think about our tiny medieval village in Tuscany. It sits high on a hill so lookouts could be placed at ramparts, watching for the first sign of approaching threat. There are two gates at the main entrance since the earliest constructed gate was deemed not strong enough by the Sienese allies. They built an even more impenetrable entrance in front of the old one, with a door that could be shut when a threat was detected. A high wall made of stone surrounds the village. Inside the village, there are iron bars on the windows, and the sturdy wooden shutters close securely, making access through the windows all but impossible. The construction of these fortifications happened over a period of a few hundred years, and they were necessary in the days of old.

Nowadays, the great door that once shut the town up is gone, allowing free entrance in and out, yet the high circling wall and the ramparts remain, along with the bars on the windows.

The danger faced by residences of Montefollonico during earlier times is evident in our own large wooden entrance door. Iron spikes jut out defensively, and opening the door involves an iron bar that must be wiggled out

of three iron loops that hold both doors latched together, able to withstand a battering ram. These medieval holdovers are strange and out of place in a day and time when they are no longer needed. Now they are simply architectural relics.

These ancient protections are a part of modern-day Italy, and it occurs to me that we do the same to our own hearts. We build defenses for a serious threat, but as time goes by, we don't take the ramparts down. We learn to live with them, dark and heavy as they are, a block to the sunshine and light, and to freedom.

I wrap my fingers around the iron bars of a second-floor window and peer through them to the panoramic Tuscan countryside beyond. It feels like the jail my mother has feared I would be thrown into all along.

"Can we take these off?"

"Someone could crawl on the roof and break in," Rocco hedges, although he admits that there's no architectural reason to keep the bars. I don't often go against Rocco's advice, but it seems unbearable to view the beauty of the landscape through iron bars, especially after working hard to liberate my own inner fortress.

Since the bars are decorative, we compromise by leaving them on one downstairs window that faces the street. Glorious freedom is imparted to the other windows, and I can almost hear them breathe a sigh of relief.

CHAPTER

No 17

E ach one is handmade," Giacomo translates as we
watch the bearded owner of a terra-cotta factory
grab a handful of gray clay from the pile and use
the palm of his hand to press the soft clay inside a
rectangular mold. He pulls a wire across the top to skim off
excess and then flops it out onto the floor in line with others.

"I thought the clay would be red, like the terra-cotta."

"It will be red after it is fired. The intense oven heat brings
out the richness and the beauty," Giacomo explains. "First it
must dry out. Ash is sprinkled over the clay, and in the heat,
the ash makes pockets in the tile to give it the old look." I don't
know how many tiles we need for our house, but to mold, dry,
and fire each one by hand seems a herculean task.

From terra-cotta, we shift our focus to travertine, as I am
told a Tuscan house must have travertine in the bathrooms.
There is a factory in Asciano, and we pass one quarry after
another with mouthlike gaping holes in the earth before we
finally pull into the parking lot. We follow Rocco and Giacomo as they skirt the office area and head straight for the factory with the purposeful steps of people who have been here
before. There we are introduced to the owner, who shows us
a specific stack of beige travertine squares.

"*Sconto*," Rocco says with a significant sparkle in his eyes. Discount. Apparently, someone from Australia ordered them and then didn't take receipt. The factory is stuck, and they need to move them.

I am perplexed as to why it's necessary to have stone on all the bathroom walls, but it seems that's what Tuscans do, so we seal the deal on the discounted stone with a handshake.

Before we leave, we are invited to come and watch the process of a chunk of stone being shaped and cut into usable pieces. The heavy stone is carried by massive cables, suspended in the air, and brought to the place where a great sawing machine begins the work. We stand a good distance back. It's noisy and violent as the cutting begins, but just as the intense heat will turn the gray clay into a red terra-cotta, so this awkward boulder will be turned into something beautiful. It is messy work, this act of creating beauty.

Trials, problems, and losses, along with the hard work of diving into the pain to find the source of false beliefs, or even sin, sometimes result in what feels like the heat of a red-hot oven or a cut from a stone saw, slicing through the hardness of our hearts.

It is necessary for beauty to emerge, but like that painful cutting of every fourth cluster of grapes to make the remaining clusters even sweeter, it takes courage.

∽∾

A daylong hike on the trails around Montefollonico seems the perfect antidote to dusty factories. We follow a path that leads steeply down the mountain and into fields of wildflowers.

If I had to choose only two flowers that remind me of this ancient place, it would be the red geranium in terra-cotta pots and the red poppies that bloom in spring meadows, for red is the color of Italy. But if red is the color of Italy, yellow is the color of Tuscany—from the golden honey-colored stones, to the yellow broom brush that flowers in the spring and brushes against our

legs when we walk, to shades of yellow on exterior and interior plaster. It's in the lemon trees and the sunflowers. It's in the golden sunshine at midday and shimmering against the hilltop villages at sunset.

"I think that's where Sofia lives." I point up a hill where a gate is open, leading to a house beyond. Sofia is a new friend, introduced by Francesca and Benedetta. In our one meeting with Sofia, she plowed ahead in Italian so fast I felt as if my brain might explode trying to keep up.

"Let's stop and see her. She invited us."

"We think she invited us. We're not totally sure what she said."

He is already halfway up the hill, the open gate an invitation—at least in Jess's mind. I chase after him.

A dog barks when we arrive. His tail is wagging despite the racket he is making, so I shift my gaze to the shadowy shape ambling toward me from the right. It's a goose. A very large goose. I've collected a menagerie of animals in my lifetime—goats, donkeys, llamas, horses, fish, dogs, and cats—but I've always steered clear of large birds. I once ran for my life from an angry male swan. I survey my surroundings for possible escape routes in case Sofia isn't home.

The door opens, and Sofia's face lights up with a broad smile. She is petite, with short, gray, no-nonsense hair. She has the olive coloring of so many Italians, and she looks as if she has been working in the garden. She waves us inside, takes us through her house, shows us photographs, hands us glasses of prosecco—all while speaking nonstop in staccato Italian. We nod, say "*sì*" several times, and ask the occasional question using the trick of one Italian word and a lilting voice.

Though the language is a barrier, visiting her home tells me she has a tender heart toward all living things. She shows us her henhouse and tells us the name of all her feathered and nonfeathered friends, which include the dog and several cats. I can sense her soul is content, living alone on this farmstead, despite a past marriage and lost love.

We tell her she must come to our house, then leave with the delighted feeling of having made a connection with another new friend. The opportunity for new friendships is endless in this magical place.

$$\sim\!\!\!\infty\!\!\!\sim$$

"Howdy doody!" Julia greets us. It's a joke now, but she used to think that was a friendly American greeting. I clarified that *Howdy* is okay but *Howdy Doody* refers to an antiquated western greeting along with a TV show from the 1950s.

We have had more than one laugh over our cultural and linguistic differences, and yet we have so many commonalities. Julia has dubbed us *cugini*, the Italian word for cousins, and our British-American friendship has already grown deep roots in this Italian soil.

Our conversation is rooted in our appreciation for the land's offering in food and wine and for the communal advantages of village life. We have shared interests in our current remodeling projects and also an admiration for Italian architecture, gardens, and art.

Our relationships with Rocco and Giacomo have also deepened. We are beginning to really know them and they us because of the amount of time we spend together, talking work but also sharing about our faith and family.

$$\sim\!\!\!\infty\!\!\!\sim$$

The bells peal for Mass at ten thirty in the morning and are heard throughout the village as a call to worship. I pad barefoot across the room, search for shoes, and find them in the dark recesses of the wardrobe. I meet Jess at the door, and we walk at a relaxed pace up the hill to the service. We are Protestants, but the appeal of a short walk to a church where we will see friends and neighbors is strong.

On other weeks we drive across the valley to Perugia and attend Giacomo's church, where the services are more rousing than our local Masses. We don't understand the language in either church, although the service order is more familiar to us in the Protestant church. Either way, it is a gift to be in a space where time is set aside for prayer, praise, thanksgiving, and meditation.

Today is a special day. There is a parish lunch in the priest's garden after church. The priest, Don Carlo, is from India, a place Jess and I have both visited. We talk of India sometimes when we meet him in the market, and his face brightens when he speaks to someone who knows his home country. He is well loved by the community, even though some say his Italian accent is *terribile*, but this pronouncement is always delivered with a heave of affectionate laughter.

The priest's garden is behind the church and has the same view overlooking the Val di Chiana as our new house. It is hidden behind an iron gate that gives only glimpses from the street of what is beyond. We file in, one by one, purchasing our tickets that will benefit the parish as Don Carlo welcomes everyone, calling each person by name, even us *Americani*.

There is an atmosphere of reserved politeness as we look around and greet some people we know and many we don't. A tent has been set up to offer shade on this sunny May afternoon. It is a festive occasion, and it seems the whole village has turned out for lunch on the grounds, whether they attended Mass or not. There is a call for everyone to take a seat, and Julia motions for us to sit with them at a table of English-speaking Italians and expats.

The table has been preset with Styrofoam plates, plastic forks, and paper napkins. There are plastic cups and clear pitchers of red wine—Vino Nobile, of course. This is no Baptist potluck.

Don Carlo takes a microphone and welcomes everyone before asking a blessing on the meal. As soon as he finishes, mothers and their teenage daughters file out the back door of the parish hall balancing trays of antipasti and place them on each table. We sit for a moment and gaze at the artistic display of cured salamis, prosciutto, and pecorino cheese.

"*Buon appetito*," Trevor says, the polite Italian call for us to begin eating.

Someone pours drinks and the conversation flows. The atmosphere of polite hellos has now transformed into engaged conversation. No one is rushed, and we take our time nibbling on the antipasti. This event is the only thing any of us have to do on this warm spring afternoon.

When trays of antipasti are cleared away, out come the ladies again, this time with plates of *pici* with tomato sauce. The fresh tomato sauce contrasted with the starch of the pasta is simple but delicious. I could eat the whole plate, but I pace myself, knowing more food is coming in the traditional Italian four-course lunch.

Suddenly, a cry rings out from a table near the front. We turn and look to see what has happened. Two ladies with frightened faces are leaning over someone on the ground. The conversation stops, and there is hushed silence as we hear frantic voices and a yell for someone to call the paramedics.

"Who is it?" we murmur at the table. We hear down a chain of whispers that it is Sofia, our new friend from down below the village. She is unconscious. I begin praying silently for her. In fifteen minutes, the ambulance arrives. A gurney is brought into the parish yard, and she is loaded onto it, somewhat conscious now. We all sit in stunned silence as the ambulance drives away, siren blaring.

The meat course is served, the dessert, and then coffee, but the party is already over, and no one has much appetite. We file out of the priest's garden with one less parishioner.

That afternoon, Jess and I take a long walk, passing by Sofia's house as if hoping to see some sign of her and praying for her as we step through the spring grasses and poppies.

The next day, Francesca tells us Sofia is recovering in the hospital. We don't understand exactly what caused the collapse, but we are assured that it isn't anything serious. I feel a weight inside me lift, and I realize that we have gone a step deeper in this community. Connecting to friends means visiting them, praying for them, celebrating with them when things go well and grieving with them when they do not. There is a responsibility to friendship, to loving others. Lowering the walls around our hearts will let in both joy and pain.

CHAPTER
№ 18

While remodeling work continues in Tuscany, summer blossoms in Kentucky and, with it, my courage to finally develop a plan to pull away from the day-to-day operations of our downtown businesses. It comes in the form of a reorganization that provides supportive services to the businesses and a new operations person to take charge.

This is wonderful news for me; I have longed for this moment, yet in the midst of it, I worry that while I am flourishing, something will be lost in transition. I spend hours writing down all the things I want to pass on to my successor so my "children," these businesses I founded, can thrive along with me. Despite my fears and concerns, the sweet anticipation of my new life will allow me to focus on the things I enjoy most with creative vision and design. This is finally the step I wanted to take when I turned fifty, the letting go of all the things that drain me, an embarkation into a new life, a new season.

While I am furiously making notes about the businesses for my successor in the early mornings, I spend the days harvesting and canning green beans and tomatoes, making blackberry jam, and pulling weeds. One morning, I go out to the goat pen to check on a sick goat. As I comfort her, her male twin is overcome with jealousy and pushes her toward me. My feet are not planted firmly, and the unexpected nudge knocks me backward onto the hard ground, where I catch my fall with my right arm.

Something is not right. My wrist hurts badly, and by noon the pain aches deep in the bone. An X-ray confirms a fracture. It will be in a cast for three weeks and the timing is rotten. I need my right arm for gardening and canning season. Even worse, we are only a couple of days away from the opening night of *Granted* at the Pioneer Playhouse, a local summer stock theater. They adapted all three of my books into plays, and this is the final one. I am supposed to be greeting readers and theatergoers each evening, shaking hands, and enjoying this last time to see my characters on stage.

Two weeks into the misery and near the end of the play run, I complain wildly to the doctor that my cast is too tight. My arm is swelling around it. He examines my arm and looks at me sternly.

"What have you been doing with this arm?"

"Nothing—much. Well, a little canning and gardening."

"I'm going to take the cast off and put you in a brace, but you have to promise not to use this arm."

"I promise!" Anything to be free from the wretched cast. I vow to let Jess help me with the canning from now on and promise to be a good girl.

By the time an August trip to Italy rolls around, I am keeping my word and letting Jess do the heavy lifting at home. However, he won't be going on this trip to check on the progress of the house, so I ask my daughters if they would like to travel with me instead. It's an opportunity for the girls to see the house for the first time. The help with my luggage will be appreciated as well so I can keep my word to the doctor.

A week before we are due to leave, an opportunity pops up. Leigh, our youngest, is accepted into a perfume course in Grasse, France, beginning in January. Her dream is to be a part of the perfume business, so this is great news. Even better, our Italy trip coincides with an opportunity for her to see an apartment and firm up plans for enrollment.

I suggest she and Adrienne take a short trip in the middle of our week in Italy to drive to France and see the apartment. After all, GPS puts the two locations five hours apart, shorter than our drive to Atlanta. No big deal. They both agree, but I ignore what I now know was hesitation on Adrienne's part. I book a nice hotel for them, feel really good about the way I have killed two birds with one stone, and feel slightly envious of their road trip adventure.

We traipse through the house in progress, and they are delighted with everything, especially the view. I am warm with their praise and affirmation. I want this to be enjoyed by our whole family, for them to feel a part of it too.

We enjoy a full day in the village together before the Monday drive to France, but I sense Adrienne's anxiety over the trip is increasing. She also knows she's likely to drive most of the way since Leigh long ago gave up cars as her primary transportation, preferring instead the life of a city dweller and public transportation.

"You will be fine. I wish I could go too!" I tell Adrienne, trying to buoy her spirits.

And I do. I love an adventure with an open road and an unknown destination, but I have to stay and help with the remodel. I rent them a car in Arezzo, and we drive there together, cutting forty-five minutes off their trip, leaving them four hours and fifteen minutes on their own. Or so we think. I wave them off with promises to keep in touch along the way.

While they are gone, I get short updates. They have arrived, but it takes seven hours. They are tired but have a good dinner. Silence, and certainly no color commentary. Something is wrong, I can sense it. Finally, a text saying they are making good time coming back.

I meet them in Arezzo, and the tension between them is thick as molasses. The trip was harder and longer than we anticipated. They report on tunnel after tunnel and bridge after bridge to cross. They are both exhausted from it, but there is more left unsaid.

We have dinner that night at the closest restaurant. We place our order when the brewing conflict between the girls bubbles to the surface, and I'm suddenly aware the stress of the trip was far harder on them than I realized. I feel responsible for the eruption and recognize how I missed cues telling me that I needed to let them make their own decisions. I took too much responsibility to solve a problem that wasn't mine to solve, a long-ingrained habit.

Striving, reaching, and performing.

Controlling.

Yes, the ugly side of solving problems is trying to control—outcomes, people, the amount of pain that might be inflicted. Sometimes even trying to control God.

In my quiet time the next morning, I confess my own contribution to their conflict—not recognizing they are no longer teenagers, trying to solve problems that are not mine to solve. God have mercy and bring on the pruning. I need it.

I run into Julia on the street the next day and invite her and Trevor to dinner with us at Il Mulino. I want the girls to know our neighbors, but we also need the dilution after the stressful night before. We walk down to Il Mulino and sit outside under the horse chestnut trees at *tavolo numero due*, our favorite table. It is a clear August night, and the sun is setting across the valley toward Montalcino.

We decide to experience a multicourse dinner with wine tasting, and since Trevor is taking some wine courses, he gives us a lesson on each wine that accompanies each course of delicious food.

Julia's quick-witted dry humor has us all laughing, which is a medicine-like balm after the difficult night before. We spend hours at the table, and by the time we get up to leave at the end of the meal, my side is hurting from the constant belly laughter.

We walk back to the village under a brilliant star-studded night sky and muse on the names of the planets and stars as we climb the hill. When we part ways inside the village gate, I know that the friendship bond with our British *cugini* has now been transferred to our daughters. I also understand the power of breaking bread together, of the restorative power of coming together at the communion table, especially when there has been conflict.

That night was a turning point in our family relationships, one that marked the beginning of growth for all of us, even those who weren't there as witness to it. My childhood experience taught me that conflict was painful and must be avoided. Now I know it is not only good but necessary.

Despite the growth conflict can create, I still ponder the lesson of trying to manage everyone else's life and how that can have damaging effects. A chilling reminder jars me when I see the news a week after we return home.

The Morandi Bridge in Genoa collapses, killing forty-three people. It was the same bridge my daughters drove over twice, from Italy to France and back.

CHAPTER
N̲o̲ 19

Our hopes for actually moving into the house on this January trip are dashed as soon as we arrive and take our first walk through. Instead of light fixtures, we have dangling bulbs. We still need cabinets, doors, and shelves.

But it's hard to stay disappointed long in Italy, especially with the festive air of Christmas lingering like the fog that sometimes hangs over the village in early mornings. We have arrived in time for the Feast of Epiphany, the celebration of the magi's visit to the baby Jesus, marked on the twelfth day after Christmas. In Italy, it's also when La Befana, a sort of good witch, follows the wise men, gets lost, and drops off presents to Italian children instead.

We have not received gifts from La Befana, but we do fill our bags with Christmas treats from the store, including bread and cookies sweetened with dried fruits and nuts.

Strings of white lights crisscross the village streets from house to house. Not only are we stocked with treats, but we are also booked for a party at the restaurant in the center of our tiny piazza, to celebrate the end of our project with all the workers who made their mark on the house. Even though the

project is not quite done, we are down to a couple of subcontractors, and all our other workers have moved on to other jobs. It's our final thank-you for all the hard work they've done for us.

Rocco, Letizia, Giacomo, and Miriam arrive early. Letizia, whom we have met a few times, is the bubbly, adorable wife of Rocco. Now she walks around the house, bragging on the work, amazed by the artistry. She might be close to sixty, but she looks like an eternal American homecoming queen with her curly brown hair, ready smile, and charmingly upturned nose. Miriam is radiant and smiling. She admires the work as well, and both Giacomo and Rocco are puffing up like peacocks with the valuable praise from their wives.

After the tour, we hold hands and offer a blessing on the house, both in Italian and in English. We pray it will be a place of relaxation, healing, and restoration to our friends and family, as well as our ministry partners.

We light a fire in the fireplace to ward off the chill so the workers can parade through the house in comfort, showing off their hard work to their spouses. It is nice to see them scrubbed clean in pressed clothing with lovely ladies on their arms.

We are given a plant from one couple, and our electrician and his wife give us a bottle of their olive oil. After everyone has walked through and admired the work, we file up to the piazza to the private room we have booked in the upstairs of the restaurant. We've asked our friends who own the restaurant to pull out all the stops and serve their best meat and wines to demonstrate our appreciation to our new friends who have contributed to our new home. It is a feast in every sense of the word.

Near the end of the meal, I look around the room and gaze at the faces of the workers I have seen leaning over stones, wires, pipes, wood, and rubble with focus in their eyes and expertise in their hands. I am filled with gratitude for their skill and labor. I take pictures of each person so I can remember them on this night of celebration.

We end the celebration with Jess expressing appreciation to them for their good work. Each couple receives a gift from us—a handmade lotion and soap from my store—and a gift from Rocco, an Italian Bible. As midnight approaches, we are all sated and happy, and we say *grazie* and *buonanotte* as each couple fades into the night.

∽

After the celebration, there are many things on my to-do list. Getting sick is not one of them. When nausea and fever hit, I collapse on the couch for two days. Jess asks Maria, the pharmacist, what to do and she sends him back with medicine. Francesca and Benedetta also offer their advice on potions and teas to fix my problem. If one has to be sick, it is best to be in a small town where everyone is concerned and trying to help. About the time I rise from the stupor, Jess falls ill. I doctor him with the same medicines and brews. All in all, we've lost four days between us to a virus, but we have been cared for by the community. When we return to circulation, we are lavished with housewarming presents. Francesca gives us a ceramic dish she made. Julia and Trevor give us handmade iron trivets from Pienza. Our other neighbors give us their homemade Vin Santo.

It is our last night in Montefollonico on this whirlwind winter visit, and we invite Francesca, Benedetta, Trevor, and Julia for an *aperitivo* in the upstairs kitchen of the new house. There is scant furniture, the couch is still covered in plastic since there will be more dust before it's over, and we gather on rickety chairs left over from Gaetana's collection.

As I prepare the meats and cheese on a platter, I wonder how often Gaetana hosted people in this room from the time she renovated the hayloft into an apartment in 1952. For eleven years it sat silent, but now it will once again be filled with conversation and joy.

Our eclectic furnishings matter not to the guests. There is laughter and nonstop talk ringing from the rugless room and bouncing off the terra-cotta. We stay up far too late despite an early flight the next morning, but we have christened our new home with good food, friends, and laughter.

As we scramble in the early morning hours to throw the last items in our suitcases, I feel a sadness about leaving Francesca's apartment. Even though we are moving down the street to our very own home, her apartment has become a sweet place of respite for us and the site of so many good memories.

In the dark of the predawn morning, after we zip luggage and Jess leaves to bring the car, I walk around the apartment and press each room into my mind. I will no longer settle into this place as if it is my own, and yet it was so significant in bringing me to this village.

The pictures we saw online drew us here so I could write my second novel, yet I could not have imagined back then how this place would change our lives. I pause in the bathroom, open the shutters, and lean out into the crisp morning air. This window was my first view to a community I now love and call my own. It was my first view of the sunset on Montepulciano and to the morning rhythm of village life. It was a whispered hope for rest, renewal, and reconnection in my marriage, my creativity, and my spiritual life. A window to a new perspective.

CHAPTER
№ 20

Il Mulino has sold to one of the American cooking schools. It will now be the base for their clients, but they will continue to run the hotel and restaurant. Along with this change, we find out the Monte dei Paschi bank branch is closing. The bank branch closing hits me hard since it is such an important anchor for the community. Yet my husband and his team have had to make the same hard decision to close branches of their bank in tiny towns in Kentucky as well. One of the branches they shuttered was in a community my ancestor founded, so it was particularly painful for me, yet I know these things must be done in order for companies to remain healthy and able to serve customers in new ways.

This is a common problem for small towns everywhere. Italian homes sit empty inside medieval walls as young people leave for employment opportunities throughout Europe and the rest of the world. These changes in Montefollonico have me thinking about how we can help the local economy in a positive way.

Jess and I have invested heavily in revitalizing our own small Kentucky town, so we are keenly aware of the need to support local small businesses. If the locals in our town didn't support our businesses, there is no way we could keep them going.

Instead of charging a rental fee for the house, we will ask our guests to support the local businesses, buy groceries from the *alimentari*, dine in the local restaurants, set up wine tastings with the local winemaker, drink coffee at the bar, and purchase art and ceramics from Francesca. In this small way, maybe we can help keep the local economy thriving.

At the same time as we are experiencing changes in Montefollonico, I am noticing some disturbing changes with my mother as well. Her memory is slipping a bit; she repeats stories and fails to recognize people she doesn't see very often. Her mind has always been razor-sharp, so while this is not a dramatic shift, it is enough to be jarring.

She had a bout of pneumonia at the end of winter, and she is physically weakened as well. Traveling from the bedroom to the living room is now precarious for her, not to mention trying to make meals or do other simple chores. It is a challenge to stay ahead of her problems, to anticipate what she needs, so we now have a granddaughter who has agreed to sleep at her house most nights.

Her ever-present fears have grown even larger and anxiety plagues her. Does she sense her mind is slipping? I have never been old, so I can't imagine all the dangers my mother perceives now that she is more dependent on others.

Though she is not back to where she was before the pneumonia, she is doing better when my trip to Italy rolls around in March. Our first set of guests is arriving soon, and the house must be furnished and ready for visitors.

Jess decides to stay home on this trip so he can stay close to my mother, which gives her great comfort. This trip is pure work anyway—more rooms to furnish, boxes to unpack, beds to make.

What I do need is another hardworking woman. I call my cousin Mary Ann, who is happy to help and excited for a trip to Italy when I suggest it. She is like a sister to me—we were both late-in-life babies to our mothers, and we spent much of our childhoods together since her mother often babysat me when my mother worked. Mary Ann is the kindest person I know, and we have always shared an easy companionship.

Besides being a good companion and helper, Mary Ann needs Italy. Her entrance into her fifties is under the shadow of divorce, the traumatic slice into the bond of an almost thirty-year marriage to her high school sweetheart and the father of her two children.

We make plans for her trip, but we decide to fly separately since I am going first to France to see our daughter Leigh, who was accepted into the perfume school in Grasse. Then I will drive the six hours down to Tuscany, where Mary Ann will meet me a few days later.

∽◡◠

I didn't marry until I was thirty-two years old. Prior to that, I traveled all over the United States by myself for my job, loving my independence, hailing taxis in big cities, and driving rental cars in remote areas, all before cell phones and GPS. Somehow, the last twenty years of marriage and traveling with my husband has created a dependence on Jess that I didn't realize I'd developed. As I wait to board the first of two planes, I feel a slight sense of vulnerability without my husband to lean into. Another woman stands alone, so I ease over next to her, and she smiles at me.

"Where are you from? Where are you going?" We make small talk, and then another woman joins us. It's simple travel chat, but there is a reassuring subtext: We are watching out for one another. This sisterhood of lone travelers reminds me that God provides not only in the spiritual realm but also in the physical.

My visit with Leigh in France is brief but fulfilling. We celebrate our March birthdays together over dinner and stay in a hotel, which gives her a break from her tiny claustrophobic apartment. We linger over a final long Sunday afternoon lunch and hug goodbye in midafternoon. It's not the ideal time to start a long drive in a foreign country, but it can't be helped. I was not about to rush out early in the morning when my time with Leigh is so short.

The GPS says I will be on the road for six hours from Grasse to Montefollonico. The drive doesn't bother me, but I do fear car trouble or a flat tire.

The emergency lane in Europe is about a yard wide, or so it seems. I really don't want to be stranded on the side of the road, especially after dark.

All does not go well. The French president is visiting Nice as I am trying to make my way through. The interstate is closed down for his security, which confounds my GPS. After thirty minutes of frustration and confusion, I finally decide to wait for other cars that seem to want to go where I am trying to go, then follow them on the unmarked detour. Ninety minutes later, I emerge on the other side of Nice.

To distract myself from the angst, I use the time to pray and then listen to an audiobook. The exit to Monaco whizzes by as a Maserati guns past me with its roaring motor. I cross the border into Italy without fanfare. There's no more than a simple welcome sign, as if I had crossed the state line into Tennessee.

As I approach Genoa, a large northern Italian port city, dark is falling. There is a detour around the collapsed Morandi Bridge, which I have managed to hit at rush hour. For another ninety minutes, I sit in dark tunnels and on bridges while Jess talks to me on the phone, checking on my progress and encouraging me from the other side of the world. When traffic finally begins to move and I make it to the other side of the city, I see the ghostly skeleton of the Morandi Bridge, suspended in midair and stopping abruptly halfway across the chasm. I shudder and keep driving.

Breaking out of Genoa gives me a sense of freedom and hope that the remaining drive to Tuscany will have no more detours, despite the lost three hours. I take only necessary bathroom stops, buy junk food from Autogrills, and throw back numerous espressos.

When I see the sign for *Toscana*, I feel as if I am coming home. It's midnight when I finally pull into Montefollonico, exhausted and drained but giddily relieved. I unload the car in front of the house, then park outside the village. When I finally shut the house door behind me, all the espressos drain from my body, and I want nothing but sleep.

The bed for my future bedroom has not yet arrived, so I must stay upstairs in Gaetana's room, and this seems a very fitting start to my first night in her house. The bed cover is dusty from the last two months of work, but I am too tired to wash it now. I am barely able to wash my face and take off my clothes. I fold the dusty bed covering down and crawl under the remaining covers. Before I drift off, I whisper a prayer of thanks to God for the safe trip, and then I thank Gaetana for sharing her beautiful home with me.

∽

The next morning, I fiddle with the gas stove until flames lick the underside of the moka pot. In a few minutes, coffee is gurgling and I pour a strong antidote to yesterday's long drive.

Coffee cup in hand, I walk slowly through the house, pausing in each room to take in all the details. The house needs much in the way of furnishing, but the renovation is finally done, and the whole building is finally up to code. No more *molti problemi*. We are two months short of two years since we saw the house for the first time, but the actual work took exactly one year from demolition to now. Thanks be to God, we are finished.

I finish my tour in the entrance room, where boxes are stacked like a small mountain in a corner, ready to be opened. Francine, an English-speaking neighbor who has agreed to help me on-site with the house, received all the boxes for me and had them placed and ready for me to tackle. Next to this mountain is a hill of bedding to be washed. Two suitcases stand bursting with items from home that I need to unpack.

I squint down at the paper Francine left for me that explains the recycling schedule. Cardboard day is Monday—*today*, I realize with a start. If I don't break down all these boxes before one thirty this afternoon when the recycling truck comes around, they have to sit somewhere in the house for another week. I take a last gulp of coffee and get started.

We decided to make the house function as two separate units, with an upstairs guest apartment and the downstairs living quarters. This means I have two washers that are now sloshing at full tilt for all the linens I brought over. A stack of new dishes needs to be washed before I put them away, so I crank up both dishwashers. Suddenly, the lights go out and everything comes to a silent halt.

Francine arrives and educates me on kilowatts. Every Italian house is allowed to have three. You can apply for six fairly easily, but there is a longer process to get ten, which is what we need with two units. I wonder why I am only now finding this out.

We call the electrical company so she can make the application for six kilowatts, which will take effect about the time I leave. After we receive this, we will then apply for the ten kilowatts, since it is somehow impossible to go from three to ten.

The village electrician shows me how to restart the electricity, since it is likely to overload several more times until the electricity is upgraded. In the meantime, I can only use one or two appliances at a time.

❧

The next day, I meet with Alberto, the woodworker, and Giacomo to discuss the remaining items that need to be finished. I find this final punch list in all projects to be the most frustrating part. We are so close, yet everyone has moved on in their heads to other tasks, and the small details that are incredibly important to me fall by the wayside.

I explain to Alberto that I would like hooks on the back of all the bathroom doors. Giacomo translates my request to Alberto.

Alberto's eyes widen in alarm. *"Le mie belle porte!"* My beautiful doors!

Giacomo explains in Italian that this is quite an American thing, to place hooks on the bathroom doors for towels and robes. Alberto finally acquiesces, saying he will do the work after we leave.

A few months later, I return to find the hooks on the wall instead of the back of the doors.

CHAPTER
№ 21

After a few days of unpacking, organizing, and running up and down terra-cotta steps, my legs are aching, making sleep difficult. I've lost weight, since there's hardly time to eat with all that needs to be done. Even though Mary Ann is on her way to help me, I want things in some order before she sees the house for the first time.

Headboards and beds have arrived for the downstairs, and all the bedrooms begin to take shape in the nick of time. I move downstairs and take over my bedroom, preparing the other guestroom for Mary Ann.

When she walks out of baggage claim at the Rome airport, we squeal and hug. She has a beautiful smile, almond-shaped eyes, and light brown hair that hangs to her shoulders in a soft cut. She looks rested despite just having slept in the seat of an airplane for the past eight hours.

We talk nonstop on the drive, and as we pull into the village, her eyes take in everything. We stop at the restaurant in the piazza for our first meal before even going to the house, since we are both famished. When the waiter comes over, he asks if we want still or sparkling water. She looks at me and mouths, "Sweet tea?" and I shake my head.

Mary Ann chooses the fizzy water, then leans in and whispers, "I think you need to give me a lesson."

I take a deep breath and lean forward, preparing to give her a crash course in menu selection at the Tuscan table. It took me and Jess a few trips to Italy and some humorous mistakes before we made sense of these unwritten cultural rules.

"First, you place your water order: still or sparkling."

"Check." She nods.

"Then you order the food by courses, but you don't have to order one from each. These days, they won't frown if you order only a pasta dish. Salads come at the end of the meal with the second course and are considered a side dish. If you order salad, the only dressing will be oil and vinegar."

I detect a slight twitch of her nose and pause, recalling my own longing for blue cheese dressing when I traveled away from the States for the first time.

"The wine order is placed *after* you place the food order, because the choice of wine is based on the choice of food. Wine is important with a meal because it cuts the fat, or so they say. There is no iced tea, no soda, nor really any other kind of beverage at the table. It's water and wine until the coffee. But coffee comes only at the end of the meal, after dessert, because it can apparently mess with the digestion if taken during the meal.

"When you are offered coffee, order an Americano if you want something close to what you drink at home. Otherwise you'll get a strong little shot of espresso. Do not order a cappuccino in the afternoon, although a macchiato is acceptable. Milk is only for the morning because it disturbs afternoon digestion. Sugar is allowed in the espresso any time of day."

Mary Ann raises an eyebrow, and I can't quite tell if she's about to burst with laughter or exasperation. But she holds steady, so I continue.

"A *digestivo*, after-dinner drink, is sometimes recommended. Some like *grappa*, but it's strong as moonshine, so I prefer *limoncello* or *mirto*. Remember, it's all about the digestion."

Mary Ann chuckles and her eyes dance with excitement. "Wow. This is going to be fun! But what about pizza? Don't they do sodas with pizza?"

"That might be the one exception. Sodas and beer are allowed with pizza. In this area, Sardinian beer is preferred. Oh, and they won't bring you the bill until you ask for it. There is never a rush to leave your table in Italy."

"I like that," she says, grinning from ear to ear.

After a two-course lunch and coffee, we go back to the car and unload her luggage, rolling it over the cobblestones and through the city gate.

"*Ciao, Angela,*" calls a neighbor as we clatter down the street.

"*Ciao, Giuliana, come stai?*"

"*Tutto bene.*"

"*La mia cugina,*" I say, pointing to Mary Ann. Giuliana smiles and says something that I take to mean "have fun" or "enjoy your time." I nod and say "*Sì,*" and that seems to be the right answer.

"You speak Italian!" Mary Ann exclaims.

"Not even close. In the land of the blind, the one-eyed man is king." We giggle our way to the house, Mary Ann slaphappy on jetlag and me giddy with her arrival.

⤫

We get to the house, which is still nondescript on the outside and painted in a nice shade of veiled cream with a large gray stripe at the bottom, just as Francesca selected for me. It is a wallflower, blending into the line of houses, not drawing attention to itself at all except for the dramatic medieval doors, which are now thrown wide open to welcome my guest.

"Look at this wood—it's ancient." She laughs with delight.

We step through the outer door, and I open the interior door. "Oh . . ." she says, her eyes wide and mouth open. "Angela, you didn't tell me it would be like this!" She trails her hand along the exposed stones. "How old is this arch?"

"Fifteenth century, or so the local historian says."

"And the ceilings!"

"Terra-cotta."

"Is this original?" She points to the terra-cotta floor.

"New, but handmade."

She is looking at everything, laying both palms on the wooden dining room table, touching the ceramic tiles on the backsplash in the kitchen, and finally opening her arms wide when we get to the terrace, as if she is ready to receive whatever Italy may give her.

"It's so beautiful! You can see for miles. I may never leave!"

This is what I have worked for all along: for others to hold close what has ministered to me. Italy cannot solve problems, but she gives perspective, and sharing that with my guests is better than receiving anything from them.

I give my cousin a tour, and she is complimenting and asking questions. Finally, I show her to her bedroom and leave her to rest for a couple of hours.

A little while later, Mary Ann emerges from her bedroom smiling after a rest and a shower.

"The bed is so comfortable, the sheets are soft, and the shutters black out the light! It's like a cave in there."

"You need a week of good sleep." We share a knowing look. The last eighteen months have been a terrible trial for her, and the anxiety of a failing marriage robbed her of sleep. I know there have been times she was curled into a fetal position on the floor, crying out to God for help. I hope this week can be a restart for her, a springing forth of new life from the old. A rebirth. A renaissance.

"I am ready to do some work. Tell me what to do."

She dives right in, and both of us working together are a force. We fall into a routine of working in the morning and then taking an outing in the afternoon, sometimes running errands along with a little sightseeing. I take her

to Montepulciano and Pienza for tours of the cities and lunches in piazzas. She is eager to try everything. Over long lunches we talk about the divorce. Her ex-husband's life is going in a different direction now, but I suppose that is the very nature of divorce. If you were going in the same direction, there's no need to separate.

I grieve for her and for her two adult children, but I am also deeply saddened by this turn of events. Her husband was my friend. I signed their marriage certificate on that June day when we were all young and full of promises to come.

∽

Mary Ann is blossoming in Tuscany. She is talking about archeology and anthropology, things I haven't heard her speak of for twenty-seven years. Marriage, raising children, and divorce took pieces of her that I now see returning in shards to create a new mosaic, a piece of art that is even more beautiful because of the brokenness.

We are eating slices of *colomba Pasquale*, which means Easter dove bread. It's a rich, sweet loaf wrapped in beautiful paper, baked in the shape of a dove, and studded with candied fruit peels and almonds.

"Why are you working so hard on the house? You know it doesn't have to be perfect," Mary Ann says, pulling off a piece of the bread.

"I know it doesn't have to be perfect, but people are coming next week. I want it to be comfortable." Her question has flown like an arrow into the very heart of my struggle. My pathetic defense dangles in the air, shriveled and unsupported.

The definition of comfortable is where the problem lies. We had a functional kitchen, water, electricity, and beds to sleep on when we arrived. It was comfortable. But now I want it to be pleasing to the eye, to have all the details thought through and prepared for the guests so they can enjoy the luxuries

of home. In essence, I want it to measure up to my standards of hospitality. Not perfect, just *right*.

It's recorded in the Bible that Mary was sitting at Jesus's feet while Martha was running willy-nilly in the kitchen, trying to put together a meal for everyone, yet when Martha complained to Jesus about her sister not helping,

Jesus said Mary was the one who got it right, not Martha. I've always had a hard time with that parable since they all had to eat, for goodness' sake. But one day, I took a closer look and realized that there was a very important word that transformed the meaning of the story. Martha wasn't wrong to prepare the meal. Her error came in preparing a *big* meal. It had to be an extraordinary meal, an amazing meal to knock everyone's socks off. She wanted platters of food placed perfectly, along with fresh flowers and fancy napkins. This meal would make Jesus proud. She was already dreaming of how much people would enjoy what she had prepared. The accolades, especially from Jesus, would be icing on the cake.

It didn't quite happen that way. Mary was praised and Martha was chastised. Her busyness led her away from the relationships. She was banging around in the kitchen while Mary was listening at Jesus's feet to the important truths he wanted them to hear. They were truths he *needed* them to hear because his time on earth as the God-Man was coming to an earth-shaking close.

My own modern-day Mary is unknowingly shooting an arrow of truth through my stubborn heart. I want the house to be amazing. I want to go far beyond providing comfortable beds, baths, and a place to store and eat food. My list of tasks never grows smaller, because when two things are checked off, ten more are added. I'm the donkey chasing the carrot, and the carrot is always out of reach. I know this by now, yet I still listen to the tyrannical dictator barking orders inside my head.

For all the work I've done knocking down the defenses around my fortressed heart and finally examining the motivation behind my need to be busy and distracted, I am now realizing it's a pattern that feels very comfortable for me. When a little pressure is added, I simply lift my elbows and go to work.

∝⌒

While Mary Ann is packing for our trip back to Rome, and then home, I meet with Francesca, who is advising me on a table for the terrace. After our conversation, we walk to the lower terrace to admire the view, a much safer pleasure now that the new iron rail is installed and there's no danger of falling to the garden below. We enjoy the panoramic vista for a bit, and then she notices a fig tree growing out of the wall below us.

"You may need to remove this and repair the wall," she says, pointing to the fig tree.

"That's our wall?"

"*Sì*, when you buy the property, you buy the wall. This is the original wall around the city, very important."

My momentary pleasure at owning part of a medieval wall is tempered with the thought of Jess losing one of his beloved fig trees. But even more foreboding is the thought of another costly repair. I had assumed the wall was the city's responsibility.

Then I notice a scattering of stones on the ground below us. *It may be worse than an out-of-place fig tree,* I think.

"How much do you think that will cost?" I ask.

She lifts her shoulders and names a number.

I swallow hard, glad Jess is not hearing this right now.

"Who can do this work?"

"Marco can do this for you."

Marco is a firefighter, but his side gig includes trimming weeds for the village, especially in precarious places like on top of ancient walls. He's also the keeper of cisterns and will climb down inside and check them for leaks. I make a mental note to request a quote from Marco. But we need to get through the home renovation before we start repairing a medieval village wall. We still have furniture to buy.

In the meantime, I purchase an Easter cake at the market to take home as a way to soften the blow. Only then will I tell Jess we are responsible for a medieval wall.

CHAPTER
N͟o 22

We have been looking forward to this day for two years. Four sets of guests have stayed in the house since my March visit, but finally, Jess and I are here together and can stay in the house we saw for the first time on that May day two years prior. It is delayed gratification to be sure, but it is finally time for something else we have anticipated these last two years: shopping at the Arezzo antique fair.

This antique market has been held in Arezzo's main piazza since the 1960s. We've been once before, scouting it out in anticipation of the time we could actually make some selections to furnish our home after the renovations. Months ago, we saw a three-foot-high carved wooden statue of Jesus holding a lamb around his neck. It was a representation of the parable that Jesus taught about leaving the herd to go after the one lost sheep, a symbol of God's pursuing love. We admired it back then but have learned it is often good to walk away from a piece of art to make sure it is something that genuinely speaks to you.

This piece of art is still talking to us, although I worry by now it is talking to us from someone else's home. We have the perfect spot for it, a place in the entrance room that formerly held a rickety wooden cupboard. It's as if this nook had been made for this exact statue.

The day after our arrival, I set the alarm for an early hour. We stumble awake, guzzle rich black coffee, and hop in our rental car for the "under an hour depending on which way you go" drive across the valley to the hillside town of Arezzo.

Before exploring the market booths, we head straight to the antique store where Jesus previously stood in the window. I hope I haven't waited too late to answer the call.

We round the corner and there he is, glowing in the showcase window, carved and painted in intricate detail in the 1700s for a church in Naples. Inside the shop, Jess asks the price again, and the shopkeeper gives us a number substantially higher than the price she told us at the end of last season.

I fish her business card out of my purse with the previous price quote written on it.

"No, this is a mistake. Impossible," she says. "Who wrote this?" she asks, as if thinking we've pulled a joke.

"You did," Jess says.

"*Noooo*," she says, in a very nasal voice. She walks over to the statue and examines it again as if Jesus himself is going to tell her if it is okay for us to have him.

We are silent and wait. We've learned the lesson that what is impossible often becomes possible in Italy.

She turns and comes back to us. "Okay, but you are getting a very good price."

We have the carved Jesus and that's the most important thing, but we could use some wardrobes and a little work table. It would be nice to have some art on the walls too. Since antiquing is one of our favorite shared activities, we know from experience that I am drawn to furniture and books, while Jess has an eye for art.

Jesus and the lamb will wait for us while we browse the antique fair. In the meantime, we walk the distance to the center piazza where vendors are in a mazelike configuration, snaking in and out of streets that meander from the center piazza in no apparent order. Because the crowds are swelling, we decide to divide and conquer. Jess leaves his old-school flip phone at home when we travel, so we do things the old-fashioned way and pick a meeting place: under the bell tower at noon.

I am intent on my job and cover ground quickly, laser-focused on finding a small table and a couple of wardrobes. When we meet under the bell tower, Jess's face is animated with excitement. He wants to show me his favorite pieces of art, but first, I lead him to the furniture I am interested in buying. While I might be the finder, Jess is the negotiator.

My frugal mother used to find clothing with stray threads or loose buttons in nice department stores and then talk the salesperson into reducing the price, knowing she could fix it at home. It worked half the time, but as I approached puberty, this embarrassed me to no end. For some reason, this embarrassment still bubbles up even today, and when Jess is in full negotiation mode, I oftentimes have to walk away. What debilitates me energizes Jess. In Italy, you are hardly respected if you don't haggle, so I have learned to overcome my embarrassment and stay for the show.

When Jess proposes a price, the dealer's no is accompanied by dramatic facial expressions and hand gestures that might be used to stop a car. The dealer writes down and circles a counteroffer. Best price. Jess tries again with a questioning stare, and there may be a slight budge, but usually the circled price is the final amount. He then tries to get something else thrown in to sweeten the deal—free delivery or another small item. I can't imagine getting these deals on antiques at home, although I am gently reminded by my banker husband of the current unfavorable difference in euros to dollars.

It is near lunchtime when we find two wardrobes that are both beautiful and useful. In true Italian style, we have built no closets in the house. Closets are not standard in Italy, where wardrobes are used to store clothes, a sensible solution that keeps clothing down to a limited number of items and keeps the floor plans for a house simple.

Jess has negotiated a price for the wardrobes and delivery from an antique dealer named Lino, but before we seal the deal, Jess suggests we think about it over lunch.

I don't need to think about it since I am already convinced these are the perfect wardrobes, but I know this is part of the negotiation process.

"Where do you want to eat?" he asks as I cut a lingering look back at "my" wardrobes.

I grab his arm. "Oh no. There's a couple looking at one of them." We dart behind a booth and watch as the two people open the doors and run their hands down the wood. Then Lino produces a measuring tape.

"It's serious. They're measuring."

"Maybe it won't fit."

We are getting looks from the owner of the booth where we are hiding, so we move on around the square, skulking between stalls, peering over at our wardrobes to watch this interloping couple. After we make a full circle, they finally walk away without exchanging money.

"Lunch can wait," I say.

We dart toward Lino and then slow our pace before entering his booth.

"We'll take them," I announce, triumphant.

"You are lucky," he says. "Another couple was just here."

"Really?"

Then Jess asks Lino if he can deliver a few more items to us from other dealers if we find anything else, since he is coming to the village anyway.

"Of course," Lino says. "If it's not too much."

By the end of the day, we add a marble-top table, a ceramic waterpot, and five chairs to his load.

Jess finds three paintings that he likes, but we carry those to the car before driving around to pick up Jesus and the lamb, waiting patiently for our return.

It's nearly ten that night when Lino arrives with the delivery. Jess helps him carry the wardrobes inside and up the stairs. When I find out that Lino hasn't eaten yet, I prepare a light dinner of *insalata mista* (mixed salad), *piselli* (peas), and a *bicchiere di* Vino Nobile (glass of red wine).

For dessert, we offer him a little Vin Santo and *cantucci*. He tells us about his family and his business in northern Italy. Jess shows him around the house and sends him off with a bottle of Brunello. Business transaction, Italian style.

∽⦿

The next afternoon, I dial up Mom on FaceTime and show her the room that we call hers, then the whole house and the terrace. She asks questions about the view, the rooms, but the art especially. She wants to see Jess's latest painting, and he holds it up for her, a sunflower in a vase sitting on a wooden chair. She gushes over it and Jess preens with her praise. My mother's desire to paint has dropped in the last year, along with many interests she used to enjoy, another sign of her diminishment.

"I can't wait for you to come on your ninetieth!" I say before we end the call. We both know it's unlikely to happen. Somehow, it makes me feel better to keep the hope alive.

After we disconnect, I walk back to the terrace to feel the warmth of the sun on my face. I feel a little sad, but the sunlight helps. While I'm there, I remember the crumbling medieval wall. I peer over the iron fence and am horrified to see the rocks have grown into an even larger pile. It's worse than I thought. I have to tell Jess immediately. If it crumbles completely, it could compromise our terrace.

I do find it is much easier to discuss unexpected expenses when he is here and enjoying the house versus back home and seeing the bank account dwindle. Our friends Wes and Roni are arriving tomorrow, and we are in high spirits. There's never a better time to break bad news than before something good is about to happen.

I make two cups of tea and find him inside, painting the background color onto a fresh canvas. It's the way he starts a new piece of work.

"I need to show you something," I say, handing him a cup of tea.

He looks up with a question, but he knows I wouldn't interrupt his painting if it weren't time sensitive. He rinses his brush, takes the cup of tea, and follows me to the lower terrace.

I point to the pile of stones below. "The wall is crumbling. It has to be fixed."

"Those rocks are out of this wall?"

"When I was here in March, there were only a few stones. It's gotten much worse in the last two months."

"How much will that cost?"

I tell him the figure Francesca quoted back in March. "That was before all these stones had fallen out."

He staggers back as if he has been shot in the chest, spilling his tea. "Are you serious?"

"We need an estimate to know for sure."

He slaps his forehead and turns to walk back up the stairs, muttering.

I see our neighbor Trevor on the street and ask him if he's seen Marco around. "He's actually working on our wall," he says.

"Can you ask him to stop by and give me an estimate to repair our section? I think it's in bad shape."

"Sure, I'll tell him this afternoon."

Marco stops by and examines our wall from above and below, then meets me on the terrace to deliver the news. Jess is painting and I'm glad he's not here.

He gives me an estimate that is a miniscule amount. This time, I am the one in shock.

"*Tutto?*" I say in amazement.

"*Tutto.*" And this is confirmed with two hands slicing through the air.

Marco leaves and I race upstairs to tell Jess. The color is coming back in his cheeks now. It's still money we didn't anticipate spending, but by comparison, this is great news.

Later, I see Julia and tell her how pleased I am that Marco can fix the wall for that price, especially with all the stones that have obviously fallen out of it.

"Do you mean the pile of stones at the bottom, love?" Julia says in her melodic English accent.

"Yes, all those rocks that have fallen out since March."

"Those stones are ours, dear. We've been piling them up there to use in the garden."

∞

We are pulsating with the excitement of sharing this new place with the Perrys. Though we've experienced trips to Italy three times before with Wes and Roni, this time they are guests in our home, but guests who have offered to come and help with whatever we need as we finish the house.

We are like excited cousins when they arrive, showing them everything and catching up with each other over long meals. Roni helps me bring back loads of red geraniums from a local nursery to plant in terra-cotta pots.

I send the guys off on a mission to buy a tiny lawn mower. We have a grassy area the size of a postage stamp, so it should be about the size of a child's toy. I emphasize this several times.

"We'll take care of it," Jess assures me.

"Tiny!" I call after them when Jess and Wes drive off, but I have deep misgivings sending a farm boy and a Texan off to buy anything small. Sure enough, when they return, Jess gets out of the car looking like a boy caught stealing. Wes averts his eyes when I give him a questioning look.

"What did you do?" I say, shifting my steely gaze back to Jess.

The pop of the trunk is the only answer. Out comes a lawn mower as big as anything I've seen in the States.

"No, you didn't. I said small!"

But there's more. Out comes a weed trimmer. Then a blower.

"Jess! And you too, Wes!" I throw my hands in the air and walk inside while I hear smothered laughter from outside. We have nowhere to put these things in this country where storage is limited. Now we have to build a shed to house equipment we don't need.

If we had room for a doghouse, Jess would be in it.

$$\infty$$

I don't let the gargantuan lawn mower get in the way of our good time with our dear friends. The week goes by far too quickly, but as their visit winds down and we see them off to Rome, we decide to open the house up to our village friends so they can see the finished product.

I send out invitations by word and text to join us for a late-morning open house. Our visitors roll in and out of the house, touring the upstairs and the downstairs over the course of a couple hours.

While our guests sip on juice, coffee, or prosecco and nibble on pastries, we hear many stories of Gaetana, how she was tall and thin, married but widowed for many years. How much she liked the mountains and how she had a chauffeur who would push-roll the car out of our current entrance room and onto the street before firing up the engine so he wouldn't disturb her upstairs.

This joyful day is the perfect way to mark our transition from frequent visitors to solidly rooted members of the community. It's a celebration with new friends in our old village, a new life given to this old house.

CHAPTER
N<u>o</u> 23

When we return home for the summer, we will bring back with us wine, vinegar, olive oil, and a teenager. Matteo is the sixteen-year-old son of Eva and Sandro, proprietors of one of the village restaurants. They want him to have an American experience and to learn English. The plan is for him to stay with us for three weeks, and then he will fly home by himself. As the date for our departure approaches, I am nervous. I lose sleep over thoughts of having a teenager for three weeks. I'm concerned he will be bored, for one thing. We don't have any other teenagers as close neighbors. My deeper fear is that something will happen to him in my care. After recently witnessing firsthand the heartbreak of a mother who lost her oldest son in a car accident, I am terrified of all the things that could happen to him while he is in my charge. I have imagined all the awful possibilities during my sleepless nights: death, broken bones, head injuries. I pray he can enjoy his time in Kentucky and that I can deliver him in one piece back to his mother. We are launching into the unknown. God be with us.

It's nearly dark by the time our plane touches down on Kentucky soil. We drive the hour south from Lexington, past green rolling hills of white-fenced pastures full of thoroughbred horses, and finally reach our farm. We are all weary from the travel, but Jess and I give Matteo a quick tour of the house, tell him to use the kitchen freely, show him the hallway bathroom, and give him the most important information: the Wi-Fi password. I've cleared out the guestroom closet and drawers in advance so he can unpack for the three weeks, but he ends up living out of his suitcase.

Matteo's English is minimal, but as with our grasp of Italian, he understands more than he can speak. He is handsome, tall, polite, and a bit shy. I imagine the local teenage girls will be starry-eyed over this young Italian.

We know a number of young people in our church and community, so I put feelers out, hoping someone will reach out to him with a social invitation while he's here so he can meet a few people his own age. We have barely landed when the invitations begin pouring in.

I find myself in the position of Matteo's social secretary, asking him if he would like to do this or that. He accepts everything. I shuttle him here and there. He goes fishing with one new friend, to the pool with another, and to the lake with some others.

Between his social activities, we are trying to learn Italian with Matteo while he learns English. He teaches us the Italian word for "cherry," but our tongues stumble over *ciliegia*, which makes him laugh. He will say "cherry" at the most unexpected moments and insist that we repeat the Italian word, but we never can seem to get it right.

Matteo's visit has coincided with Jess's annual board meeting, which involves a reception before the meeting. I explain the food at the reception, introduce him to more Americans than he's likely ever seen in his life, and explain what is going on and who these people are.

We are standing together for a few minutes when he asks me a question. "Angela, what this mean, 'boody'?"

My mind goes to the slang term for a person's backside. I've learned he likes Italian rap, so maybe he's been listening to American rap. I hesitate.

He sees my confusion, so he helps me out. "Jess calls me boody."

The light goes on and I laugh, relieved that I will not have to discuss posteriors with a teenage boy.

"Oh, yes! He's calling you buddy. It's an affectionate term, like friend, usually used with men or boys."

I am sure our Southern accents make it more difficult for him. Not unlike us learning Italian in Tuscany, this young man has the added challenge of country accents. I am getting a hint of what it's like to be on the other side of the language barrier. I can only imagine the times an Italian friend has had to refrain from laughing in my face. How many Italian versions of *boody* have I inquired after?

We take Matteo to church and sit near our pastor's family with his three beautiful teenage daughters. I am quite sure that Matteo's only religious exposure thus far has been in the Catholic faith. What must he think of our worship service, with an electric piano, drum, violin, and guitar? The lack of liturgy and the presence of a pastor without robes must seem strange and perhaps irreverent to him. Does he understand any of the thirty-minute sermon?

Anytime I'm told of the youth from church having a gathering, I ask him if he wants to go, and he's always eager. It's clear that in spite of his shyness, he is doing his best to make the most of this time in America.

While Matteo is young, vibrant, and full of life, my mother's health has deteriorated to the point that she has stopped cooking Sunday lunches. Strangely enough, I find myself a bit wistful for the days when she made her ketchup-based soups.

Now she or her helper contributes by setting the table, and I prepare the lunch. We drop it by on the way to church, and she warms it up and has it ready when we get back. She used to go to church with us, but that also stopped with this winter bout of pneumonia. Mom is not herself, and as much as I hope she will eventually come out of this, I have to recognize in spite of her youthful spirit, she is an eighty-eight-year-old woman with health issues.

Despite her physical decline, she still dresses every morning in as much bling as she can muster. Hats are generally reserved for times she goes outside the house, which have diminished in recent months, but her sparkly vests, blouses, and studded pants still circulate through her daily attire.

Now that I am cooking, our traditional Sunday lunch is a roast or a hearty beef vegetable soup. Matteo eats with gusto. He is attentive and respectful to my mother, and I can see he has been raised well in respecting his elders, with two *nonne*, or grandmothers, living with or near him. We serve pies and cakes, and he tries everything.

The only time I have ever seen Matteo not want something was the pasta I made the first week he arrived. I had imagined he missed the pasta from home, so I made a feeble attempt to imitate a dish from Tuscany. I committed the cardinal sin of overcooking the pasta, and even I didn't like it, so I can only guess what it tasted like to him.

Mexican food is a novelty. He loves tacos, burritos, tortilla chips, guacamole, and salsa, so I've been making every Mexican dish I know.

Matteo comes home from a movie one night, and he is frustrated by the popcorn.

"*Troppo burro,*" he says, expressing his feelings in Italian. Too much butter. "Why so much?"

"*Non lo so,*" I say. I don't know.

"Too many sauces in America. Why is this needed?" His question is earnest, not critical.

"I really don't know," I say. Now that I am thinking about it, I realize how true it is. We have dips for everything from chips to veggies to chicken strips.

Our salad dressings are rich and creamy and go from the white of ranch to the red of French to the yellow of honey mustard. For sandwiches and burgers, we have ketchup, mustard, mayonnaise, aioli, and chipotle sauce.

In Italy, the fresh ingredients or well-prepared meat takes center stage, subtly complemented with fresh herbs, salt and pepper, a splash of olive oil, or maybe a squeeze of lemon. No condiments with lengthy ingredient lists are needed. Maybe our love of dips and sauces is simply a way to cover up bad food.

We take a family outing to Lake Cumberland for a ride on Jess's sister's boat and some tubing for Matteo and our grandkids. The day is sunny and warm. Laughter, screams, and lots of splashing water make the day a big hit.

The following day, I come down with allergies that morph into a cold and then respiratory infection. I recognize the signs of a stressed immune system. I am run-down. It's been difficult balancing visits with my mother, work responsibilities, and hosting a teenager, on top of returning from an overseas trip, and now long-distance managing that one last building project, a shed to house our lawn equipment.

While I'm recovering, Jess keeps Matteo busy with motorcycle drives and gator rides on the farm. He has a final outing with friends, and by the time I take him to the airport for the flight back to Italy, I am on the mend. I thank God all the way to Lexington that I am delivering him back to his mother in one piece.

CHAPTER
№ 24

The house still needs work. The cantina isn't finished, and there are more shelves to be installed and empty spaces in need of furnishings. Managing the project with an ocean between us and the cultural and language differences has felt at times like trying to paint a masterpiece in the dark. We've come so far, but for every item we get crossed off the punch list, it seems another is added. It would be easy to stop here and say *basta*, enough.

I find the same is true as I work through my own emotional and spiritual journey. Maybe I've come far enough and can just call it quits on the healing and growth process. After all, it's hard work, and I'm a little exhausted from sifting through old hurts and habits, even though the rewards have been in spades. Recently, I have been feeling an unobstructed flow of love, forgiveness, and grace like never before, which has enabled me to give it back to others more fully. Pruning has allowed me freedom from many of my old responsibilities so I can embrace the gift of this new season, this new decade.

There is still my mother, her growing needs, and the gradual realization that she is not going to get better. I begin to see a counselor, who helps me talk through the lifelong feeling of never being enough for my mother, for both my parents, for not being able to solve all their problems and for thinking it was my responsibility in the first place. When my mother says, "Are you going to leave me now?" my counselor teaches me to say, "Mom, I am never going to leave you. You are always in my heart," which transforms her face into a smile. I wish I had known to say that years ago. It's true, after all.

But she is leaving me. I sense that I am losing my mother, and sadness washes over me like a pelting rain. I am not ready for her to go.

The summer before, when her mind was a bit sharper and her body healthier, we traveled to Lexington for a shopping and lunch outing. On the way home, I asked, "Mom, are you afraid of dying?"

"No, not of death. To be absent from the body is to be present with the Lord," she quoted from Scripture. "But I do fear the process."

Emboldened by this honest talk, I said, "If there's anything I have ever done to hurt you, I'm sorry, and I would like your forgiveness."

"Oh, honey, there's nothing."

Later, I got a text from her.

"I should have said the same thing to you. If there's anything I have done, please forgive me."

That was a balm, and yet I still get frustrated with her, still have feelings of guilt over not being there as often as she would like, even sadness over wanting the home she can no longer embody or provide. I can't be a teenager taking a nap on the living room couch anymore and hear her rattle around in the kitchen making supper. Those days are gone, and the ones left seem to slip away like sand through my fingers.

One day, we are talking about events from her childhood and her youth, and she says, "I probably should have seen a counselor." I suggest that she see my counselor and she agrees. "That sure wouldn't hurt."

I make an appointment for Mom with my counselor at her house. I meet him at the front door, a wiry man in his sixties, wise, calm, and funny. I introduce Roy to my mother and leave them to talk, closing the kitchen door so they can have privacy.

Laughter rings through the door, and I smile to myself as I clean up Mom's kitchen. An hour later the door opens, and they are both grinning. This is unlike any counseling session I've ever experienced, but if she's happy, I'm happy.

"We had such a good time," Mom says. She is coyly cutting her eyes at Roy. After my father died, my mother turned into a shameless flirt.

"Wonderful. Should we make another appointment?" Mom and Roy heartily agree, so we set the time for two weeks in the future: Friday, September 13.

I couldn't have imagined the terrible significance that day would come to hold.

∽◠

The following Sunday, Jess and I go to Mom's house for lunch. She is in good spirits but says her back is hurting. The caretaker is concerned about a UTI. Medicine is called in, but it is Labor Day weekend, and getting attention from doctors and home health nurses, or even medicine from the pharmacy, is difficult. She is growing sicker and weaker, but she doesn't want to go to the hospital.

By Wednesday, it is obvious she is failing. My sister and I call the ambulance, and the emergency room doctor delivers upsetting news: My mother has an obstructed bowel. This requires surgery, but she is too weak and frail. They try treating it with medicine. We are in the ICU and then out because she appears to be getting better. Suddenly, her health declines. Mom's body is septic, she is talking incoherently, and we launch into a terrible and traumatic twenty-four hours.

My sister and I spend one final night with her, taking turns sitting by her hospital bed, holding her hand, and talking to her. A couple of minutes before noon on Monday, September 9, she takes her last breath with me, her baby girl as she always called me, on her right side and her firstborn on her left.

After a few minutes of sacred silence, I begin ticking through the to-do list, reverting to my old habit of planning and work when faced with a grief or stress I cannot handle.

"Someone call Ramsey's Funeral Home."

A niece volunteers and steps out to make the call.

"Did somebody call Donna? We need to tell Idella and Betsy. Maybe Thursday and Friday for the visitation and funeral." Thoughts are flying around in my head like wildly shot arrows with no target.

"She needs a Xanax," another niece says to no one in particular.

No, I need to be alone with my mother, I think.

I have just lost my mother. The thing I have dreaded my whole life has happened to me. One by one, everyone leaves, and I am finally alone with my mom's body.

I sit in a chair away from her. I watched her spirit leave her body, and I know she is not there. There is no more comfort I can give by touching her, but somehow, I can't bear to leave her alone in this stark room to wait for the strangers from the funeral home who are coming to take her away. I sit with her, my own private little wake.

Finally, two men arrive, manners quiet and polite, and cover her with a sheet before wheeling her out of the room and down the hall. I stand in the doorway of the hospital room and watch them go, numb with shock.

Are you going to leave me now? my soul cries out.

⚬⚬⚬

I can't remember the last time I've eaten. Adrenaline, black coffee, and prayer have been my only fuel for the last day or more. I feel myself sinking under the darkness of despair and exhaustion. In the end, I couldn't fix all her problems. It wasn't enough. I was not enough.

I go home that evening to find the sink full of dishes and the dishwasher full. I mechanically unload the clean dishes and put the dirty dishes inside the machine. One minute you're saying goodbye to your mother as she slips into eternity. The next minute you're unloading the dishwasher.

"God, help me," I whisper. "I am desperate for you."

That night, I go to bed and dream the most incredible and vivid dream. My mother comes out of a hospital room pushing her walker, but as she comes toward me, she reverts to a much younger and straighter person, gaining the significant height and weight she lost with age. The rollator disappears, and she walks right up to me, straight and smiling. Then she leans down and whispers, "I love you" in my ear before disappearing.

I wake up crying. The dream is so real that I'm sure it's more than a dream. It's a vision. I weep through a prayer of gratitude.

Two days later, Friday, September 13, on the day that was intended to be her next counseling session, we follow a riderless horse that leads the walking funeral procession to the graveyard. Mom is laid to rest there next to my father and all her family members, along with all her resolved and unresolved hurts and expressed and unexpressed joys.

She didn't make it to Italy on her ninetieth birthday, dying a month after turning eighty-nine. It makes me wistful to know that we never got to walk through the house together, that she didn't see the panoramic view of the Val di Chiana from the terrace, that she didn't admire the craftsmanship that went into each stone of the house.

I wanted her to sleep in the room I set aside for her, and to bring her a cup of coffee with two spoons of sugar to sip in the morning light under the pergola. I wanted to have one last hysterical laugh over something silly, to see her shoot a flirting glance at an Italian man thirty years her junior, and for her to experience the vineyards and olive groves. All these things I wanted, but God had a different journey in mind, and Italy, for all her shades of golden glory, pales in comparison to Mom's view now.

CHAPTER
N<u>o</u> 25

O nly three weeks after I bury my mother, we arrive in the village, greeted with kisses, hugs, and heart-felt condolences. Italians revere their mothers, and these expressions of sympathy feel deeply authentic and comforting.

It is harvest season for the grapes and olives, but also for us as we reap the fruit of our labor on the house by welcoming our kids and grandkids on fall break, filling the house to capacity for the first time and using every inch of space. Our electricity has been increased to ten kilowatts, and we should be prepared for the American invasion.

We have anticipated this time for so long, dreaming and working toward the day when this ancient stable-turned-house will be filled to the brim with those we love. These precious times when the whole family can gather together are limited by work schedules and school calendars, and we are missing our younger daughter, Leigh, who can't make this trip due to a school commitment.

Laughter and voices ring through the house, and the bed situation is sorted quickly—who will sleep where and what bedding is needed for which couch. While the grandkids race around the village streets to the park and back, our adult children decide to literally run to Montepulciano, the village across the valley from us. We direct them to the *strada bianca* and they are off. "It's a long way!" I call out, but they are undeterred. They are young, healthy, and fit.

There are dinners out and dinners in, long talks on the terrace as the sun drops and the shadows lengthen. Games of Rook and Rummikub fill up hours, along with tastings of local wines for the adults.

I take walks with our two older granddaughters on the public park trails. We admire the fairyland appearance of delicate lavender cyclamen flowers in masses on the sides of the trail. Porcini mushrooms are growing in the forest, and we spot some on the sides of the path, but we leave them for an expert to identify and harvest. Chestnut trees are dropping their nuts, delicious for roasting and serving at the end of a meal or as a snack. Restaurant menus feature pumpkin and squash soups, along with suckling pig, pigeon, rabbit, and the organ meat of various animals, which Italians seem to devour.

We visit Pienza, Montepulciano, the Val d'Orcia, and the Val di Chiana. We are invited to Siena for lunch at Rocco and Letizia's home, along with Giacomo and Miriam and their new baby, Elia. It is a multihour affair, lounging under the warm autumn sun with the cozy feeling of being with family.

It should since the Sardones feel like family, after going through this house project together with us. Giacomo and Miriam came to Kentucky before Elia was born, so our son, Preston, and his family already know them. Now there is a baby for us women to cuddle and admire, and things for Preston, Giacomo, Rocco, and Jess to discuss over tiny glasses of *limoncello* at the end of lunch.

Our farmer son is deeply interested in the local farming methods. One morning, he and Jess go off to watch our village winemaker, Signor Innocenti, and his workers as they harvest the grapes in a vineyard below the village. Signor Innocenti's family and employees pick the grapes by hand, snipping the clusters with care so the grapes and vines are undamaged. He produces an award-winning Vin Santo, the envy of many large producers, which can be sampled deep in the stone cantina below his village storefront.

Larger vineyards, more interested in producing mass quantities of table wine, use machines that are driven between the rows and aggressively attack the vines to capture the grapes. Preston has spent his life's work countering the corporate treatment of meat animals; he believes in pasture-raising them instead of feeding them genetically modified corn for a quick fattening. This seems right by creation and resonates with the way Signor Innocenti picks his grapes.

It is a good year for wine, the locals say. We've had the right amount of rain in the spring, hot and dry weather in the summer, and cool weather in the fall. There is hope of this year being an excellent vintage.

The weather that makes a superior wine vintage doesn't always make good olives. The olive harvest will not be as good, the locals say. With the olives, there are similar choices on how to manage the harvest as with the grapes. The traditional method is to use ladders that lean against the tree, allowing pickers to pick or comb the olive branches gently, letting the olives fall to a net below the tree.

There are also battery-powered twizzle forks called *abbacchiatore* that vibrate the branches and drop the olives to the net below. Many large farms also use machines that open up around a tree in a net and then shake the trunk of the olive tree, causing all the ripe olives to fall. This method seems far too violent.

The week goes by far too fast, and we see our family off to Rome in the early morning hours. Jess and I wander through the quiet house, feeling slightly forlorn. We clean and straighten, laughing over a doll found behind a door and a Lego piece that shows up in the silverware drawer.

Our spirits are buoyed when we attend Giacomo's church in Perugia the next day. We take cappuccino dispensed out of a machine into tiny plastic cups in the office building lobby that transforms into a church on Sundays. As the service begins, an English speaker sits next to us to help translate, but

I like hearing the service in Italian so I can learn. We sing the songs in Italian and catch the gist of the sermon. I look around at the earnest faces in the room and realize these people are our family too. We may speak a different language and have a different culture, but we are family. Our blood relations may be an ocean away, but we can always be at home here.

⁂

A couple of days later, I am forced to take a strange detour through the village due to some road work. I misjudge the turn and hit the fender of a parked car.

I get out of my car and look around, but no one is there. I take a picture of the license plate and the damage. I don't have anything to write on, so I go back to the house and find paper and pen, then head back to the damaged car.

It's gone. I text our neighbor Trevor, tell him what happened, and send a picture of the damage on the car, thinking he may recognize it. He doesn't, but he puts the word out in the village.

By the next day, we find out through the village network that the car I have dented belongs to a man named Ricco. He blamed the accident on his wife, so now I come forth as the true culprit and hope his marriage will benefit.

Ricco and I meet on the street with Trevor translating for us. I'm expecting someone a bit irate, since I have caused him a great deal of inconvenience, and who knows what kind of marriage trouble. Instead, he is smiling, full of affability.

"I'm so sorry I hit your car! I am happy to take care of the cost of repairs," I tell him earnestly.

He shrugs and looks away, as if there will be no charge, but I have learned this is only the beginning of the conversation.

Ricco speaks a paragraph or two of Italian. I catch most of it, and he is telling his side of seeing it, thinking his wife did it, blaming her for it, and then finding out it was not his wife after all.

"Please tell your wife I'm sorry!"

We laugh and then I say, "Let me know the cost and I will pay you."

Ricco crosses his arms, shrugs, and then looks away as if he is thinking. I wait patiently.

"*Penso duecento euro.*"

"*Tutto?*"

"*Sì, basta.*" Yes, enough.

I hand him the money and we shake hands. No drawn-out estimate needed. No insurance companies.

Later that evening, Jess and I are walking around the village, and I show him the scene of my crime. We walk past the parking spot and see an open garage door where a man is leaning over a jug.

"Ricco," Jess says.

Ricco looks up and smiles. He comes over and shakes Jess's hand.

"Vin Santo?" Jess points to the jug.

"*Sì.*" Ricco's chest swells. "*Un momento.*" He disappears down some steps and then appears with a bottle. He hands it to Jess. It's a bottle of his homemade Vin Santo. Hitting someone's car has been such a pleasant experience I just might do it again.

❧

Francesca has sent me a notice of an olive oil festival in Castelmuzio, so Jess and I take back roads toward neighboring Trequanda, turning off the GPS to rely on our growing sense of direction in these wooded hills.

Castelmuzio is shining and at its best. Olive oil purveyors are set up on simple tables with their oil and some bread for tasting. Also for sale: homemade pasta, hemp soap, and a table of painted rocks being peddled by two enterprising young girls. There is a raffle for fundraising. A group of drummers marches through town, winding through the four streets that crisscross and connect to each other. One stand sells handmade baskets of colored woods, including olive wood.

We taste several olive oils and purchase our favorite, select some home-made pasta, buy a woven basket, and snack on a handful of roasted chestnuts sold by an older couple roasting them with great flourishes over a fire in an iron skillet.

We stroll down the narrow street to leave, happy and content with our outing. Out of the corner of my eye, I catch a breathtaking display of color in an artist's booth. The shadows and light of an olive grove in autumn colors perfectly capture the mood of our happy outing. I linger around in the booth, looking at other paintings, but I can't keep my eyes off the olive grove. The light draws me to it. Jess nods his agreement, and we buy the painting and leave with a harvest of memories for this day and a piece of art for remembrance.

CHAPTER
№ 26

A local cat has adopted me, which I take as another sign of my acceptance into the village. This calico comes to the terrace door every morning, peers in the window, and waits for the milk I bring her. I have been adopted by other cats before, so I understand the responsibilities. It is my job to provide her milk on demand. It is her job to grace me with her presence . . . when she chooses.

I do have a slight bone to pick with this cat. When I see her out in the village, she completely ignores me, despite my calls to her. It's as if she is embarrassed for the villagers to know that she and I have this private relationship.

I think she might express a bit more gratitude since many of the villagers employ an old trick of filling glass water bottles and placing them outside their doors to deter cats. Cats supposedly don't like the glimmering water and will stay away. I have literally thrown out the welcome mat with my daily milk deposits on the back stoop, yet she barely raises a whisker when I pass her on the street.

She is perched on a neighbor's car, watching with disinterest—one might even say disdain—as Jess and I leave our house. Two can play at this game. I ignore her as well as we walk down the street to pile into the back seat of Trevor and Julia's car. We talk and laugh as we drive into the Val di Chiana to a village called Abbadia for lunch at Sandro and Eva's house. It's a thank-you for hosting their son Matteo last June. They are taking their precious day off from the restaurant business to prepare lunch for us, and what a preparation it is.

We meet Eva's parents and Sandro's mother, who live nearby. It seems the whole family is involved in the lunch preparation. First we are handed glasses of prosecco and are seated around charcuterie boards that could be a meal by themselves.

We tour the house and grounds, which also operates as an *agriturismo*, a farm stay. We see Matteo's room with posters of gorgeous young women on the walls. His twelve-year-old brother's room is filled with games.

In the living area there is a great fireplace with bench seating, which is where the family sits, giving us the comfy chairs around the coffee table. We chat and laugh in a mix of Italian and English. The house is warm, beautiful, and comfortable. We tell stories about Matteo's robust social calendar in Kentucky, and then we ask questions of their parents. I feel enveloped into this family, a sweet and unexpected reward after welcoming their son into ours.

When our prosecco glasses are empty, we move to a long table and bench seats. The two *nonne* serve the pasta first. Two delicious red wines are paired with the courses of four meats, roasted potatoes, and salad. Then there is a dessert wine with tiramisu. It is a four-hour extravaganza, a feast of biblical proportions. I won't be able to eat for a week, but I don't regret a single bite.

∾

I sit on our terrace late one afternoon and soak up the sun since the days are growing shorter. The nearby church bells peal, creating a magical soundtrack to the view. I now understand the meaning of those bells that seem to ring different melodies at odd times of the day.

The first bells of the day toll at eight for morning prayers. Noon is the call for midday prayers. At four thirty and five, the bells are a call to daily Mass. At seven in the evening, they ring for the Ave Maria. At eight, they ring a final time as an evening call for vespers. How beautiful to live life by this daily call to prayer! I wonder how I can incorporate this rhythm of prayer in my own life at home. What are my reminders to pray at certain times of the day?

I think about the clocks I have at home. Lately, I've become dependent on my phone for any alarms needed, yet it lacks the romance of authentic bells and chimes. In my living room, there is an antique mantle clock that belonged to my grandparents. I intend to begin the ritual of weekly winding that clock so the hourly gongs will remind me to pray, even if only a brief prayer of thanksgiving.

Over the past few years, I have gradually infused my life in Kentucky with a little of the Italian culture. Now I block off two hours for a lunch with friends instead of rushing off to a meeting after one hour. I am never without Italian cheese in the refrigerator, a selection of Italian wines in the cellar, and an espresso maker ready to steam out the best Italian coffee. I try to slow my pace by lingering in conversation on the street with friends and acquaintances instead of running from one place to the other.

The secret of *la dolce vita* for me is a lingering appreciation for faith, family, food, friends, and the peace and contentment that well up when that lingering is allowed to bear fruit. This is possible anywhere in the world and certainly without restoring an ancient house.

❧

A couple of days before we are due to leave, we have one of those delicious days with no agenda. We drive into the Val d'Orcia and have lunch in Montalcino, then take back roads in the general direction of home.

The spires of a church stand above the trees up ahead and we are intrigued. We pull into a small gravel parking lot and read a green sign: *Abbazia di Monte Oliveto Maggiore*. We walk across an old wooden drawbridge and pass through a square tower, then emerge into the abbey grounds and follow a long, cypress-lined pathway. There are several redbrick buildings, and we follow signs to the great cloister, which is decorated with thirty-six immense frescoes depicting scenes from the life of Saint Benedict. This monastery was founded in 1320, we read, and the frescoes were begun in 1497 by Lucca Signorelli and finished by Sodoma in 1508. Hushed, we walk slowly around the covered portico, gazing at the walls and trying to decipher the symbols and stories the artists wanted to convey.

For a long time, I sit staring up at one of the frescoes. Tears prick at my eyes. I don't know if the art is really this good or if the beauty of the experience, being bathed in art and light, is simply magnified because of the darkness I have walked through losing my mother.

I feel a growing longing for beauty and lightness. Maybe it's maturing or being around so much death. It seems strange how many times I've had to grapple with death and seek healing from loss here in this beautiful land of Tuscany. My appreciation of beauty is heightened by the juxtaposition of the grief I've experienced, often simultaneously. Or maybe it's as the French philosopher Albert Camus wrote in one of his notebooks: "Beauty is unbearable and drives us to despair, offering us for a minute the glimpse of an eternity that we should like to stretch out over the whole of time."

On our drive home from Monte Oliveto Maggiore, I drink in every aspect of the autumn landscape. It will be four months before we return, and I'm already missing it. As we navigate the curves in this white gravel road for the final time this year, I roll down my window and let the unseasonably warm air tousle my hair. I want to absorb the sensation of being here into my skin, my eyes, my heart. My eyes take in the hilltop fortress and the valley farmhouse; they follow trailing vineyards down rolling hills; they search for darting foxes, birds, and *cinghiale* between the trees of the forest, storing away the beauty of this harvest into my mind for the long winter months to come.

I stand out on our terrace, thinking about the transformations that have occurred here, in this house and in myself. The evening light deepens over the valley before me, heightening contrasts and textures of the landscape momentarily and then softening into a faded dusky hue of purples and greens. Cortona's lights begin to sparkle and wink on the hill in the distance. I smile and turn my back on the valley views to gaze up at this ancient house we've poured so much love and care into. The renovation has given this house new life while honoring its history. But is it ever really finished? Won't there always be one more shelf to add here or a piece of furniture to place there in order to adapt the space to our needs and those of our guests as we spend time in these rooms? This is not unlike writing a book. What author doesn't want to go back and change words or sentences, even after the book is in print? This seems to be a general desire of all artists, since even Leonardo da Vinci is attributed with saying, "Art is never finished, only abandoned."

Like the frescoes I viewed at the Abbey of Monte Oliveto that tell the life story of Saint Benedict, I think about my own life frescoes and the transformation since finding myself in Tuscany. I've taken significant steps back from the hands-on role I held for so long with our businesses, encouraging others to step up and grow into new roles, which has given me space to flourish in the areas I enjoy the most. I've turned down requests that would have pulled me in other directions from the path I feel God has for me at this time. I've created margin in my schedule for the people and activities that give me life and purpose.

I've done the hard work of digging into the root of my behaviors and the lies I believed that set me running on a spinning wheel. I've read countless books on emotional and spiritual healing, journaled progress and setbacks, prayers and praise, sought counseling from others, meditated on Scripture, studied the Bible in formal studies and on my own, walked, prayed, and listened. Each moment so small in its own, and yet now that I look back at them all together, I can appreciate the cumulative effect that has brought me healing, growth, and flourishing in ways I wondered were even possible.

Though I invited the pruning process into my life, I feared the cutting of the good fruit. I wondered if I could have such courage. Now it has happened, both in ways that I chose and in ways I did not want. Surely the loss of one's mother is a cut so deep, a source of pain that will take time to heal, even as I lean in to cherish the good memories with her.

What I have experienced in my fifties has not been at all what I thought or hoped it would be. The losses and obstacles keep coming in knock-down waves, and yet the spiritual and personal growth have exceeded my wildest dreams. While I have not always felt safe, it has been good.

This coming winter, there will be another round of pruning as I go through each item in my mother's home, take time to savor the memory attached, and then decide whether to keep it or give it away. Finally, there will be the letting go of the place I called home since I was fourteen years old.

I spent the last year acquiring kitchen items, bath accessories, books, art, and furniture for this home in Tuscany. Soon I will do the opposite work on the home of my youth. One is given, one is taken away.

⚬✦⚬

Autumn bittersweet grows along the roadsides here in Tuscany, as it does on our country roads back home. The bright orange berries are eye-catching against the drab foliage, the essence of fall beauty, the prelude to the cold winds of winter.

This sweet tang of harvesttime in Tuscany is all I had hoped this place we have come to love would bring us. I didn't anticipate the suffering that would accompany it, but here we are, in this season of bittersweet.

For this moment I push aside thoughts of winter and try to remain present on this terrace in Tuscany, where darkness has fallen. With blackness around me, I am forced to look up to see the beauty of the heavens where the stars glitter and remind me of the vastness of space and the presence of God. How easy it is not to look up in the darkness.

I gaze up in gratitude for the sweetness of harvest and all that Montefollonico has come to mean to me over the years. Pots of vivid red geraniums, peppery green olive oil, Benedictine frescoes, travertine bathroom walls, cypress trees with bands of white road dust, flocks of sheep with their shepherd, a calico cat playing hard to get, ripe clusters of grapes scattered on the ground, and exquisite local wine being poured from bottle to glass.

My stomach growls as the hearty scent of ragu floats on the air from our neighbor's kitchen window. I hear Italian voices in passionate discourse and the clink of silver on ceramic dishes. Tuscany is the new oil fresh from the mill on toasted bread, a slice of porchetta with a glass of red wine, and hand-rolled *pici* pasta with fresh tomato sauce.

But more than any of those things, it is the people: Francesca working in her art studio, Carlotta cooking gourmet food in stilettos, Giacomo and Rocco giving advice on the work, Letizia and Miriam opening their homes to us, Benedetta scolding Leonardo, Julia and Trevor chatting with us over the low wall that separates our gardens, Giuseppina and her daughters serving pizza hot from the oven, Alfonso on his little green scooter-truck, and Jess painting canvases in the morning light.

Most of all, it is who I am in Italy: rested, inspired, and nourished. Pruned and flourishing.